The Beautiful Aardvark:
A veterinarian's story about creating, running and selling a small business

Workbook included so you can too...

Copyright By Dr Timothy Mann 2016
Forward by Brian Faulk 2016

www.beautifulaardvark.com
drmann@gramercyvet.com

www.timothymann.com
www.gramceryvet.com

Table of contents:

Forward — *Page 5*
   Using Analysis, Resources and Knowledge

Introduction — *Page 7*
   The AARDVARK Method and me
   Adaption, Activism, Respect, Drive
   Values, Analysis, Resources and Knowledge

Chapter One — *Page 13*
   How to train a horse
   Harnessing Respect and Drive

Chapter Two — *Page 23*
   College, Cuba and Creativity:
   Using Adaptation

Chapter Three — *Page 33*
   In Search of a Vocation
   Gathering Analysis and Knowledge

Chapter Four — *Page 47*
   Starting a Business:
   Empathetic Planning and The Aardvark Method

Chapter Five — *Page 58*
   Rebuilding Brooklyn
   How Others used the Aardvark Method

Chapter Six — *Page 67*
   Redefining Success:
   Activism as a business principle

Chapter Seven   **Page 75**
    Playing with a ball: Values in action

Chapter Eight   **Page 85**
    The Incredibles
    Animal Stories showcasing Knowledge

Chapter Nine   **Page 95**
    Selling Out: A change in culture and process

Conclusion   **Page 102**
    Putting It all Together

Workbook   **Page 107**

Foreword

Brian Faulk
Senior Lender, Live Oak Bank

As a small business lender and expert in the field, I certainly know that starting, managing or running a business is a daunting task! Nonetheless, Dr. Mann tells a great story with plenty of lessons for us all. Dr. Mann does an amazing job of using real life anecdotes and heartwarming animal stories to illustrate core principles, which are key in any business. If you aren't interested in business, then just read them and smile!

As the lender that helped fund this amazing story, I know that Dr. Mann did several things that made us believe that he would be successful and thus a great candidate for funding. As the book shows, a business owner has to adapt and innovate which takes time, energy and financial resources. I remember telling Dr. Mann that his experience as a bar tender may have taught him some important lessons, such as the value he places on all of his relationships. From his business plan to meeting in person, we saw that his relationship-driven practice was evident with his vendors, patients and staff. By focusing on authentic and meaningful relationships, he clearly lowered his costs through minimal employee turnover, and created a service-oriented practice with maximum engagement from his team and clients alike. In our experience, the most successful entrepreneurs are those who follow the lessons that are outlined in this book. The willingness to be sensitive and responsive to the needs of others and to adapt and evolve helped his practice become a blockbuster.

I hope several of you will use this story to empower yourself to take the next step and either start a business or improve your existing one. If you are going to do so, this book is a must read.

You will see how having a very strong vision with a solid business plan is essential, but being flexible or "adaptive" as Dr. Mann describes, is even more important. Working with Dr. Mann was a pleasure because you could see that he was willing to listen and adopt any advice that was given. You will learn that you need to pro-active about communication and be upfront about potential challenges so that you can defeat them, just as Dr. Mann did.

This book illustrates several principles and lessons that will make me, and any lender, want to fund your project! It is interesting to read about the other businesses and what made them succeed. By succeeding, these businesses transformed the area from empty storefronts and abandoned buildings to one with thriving bookstores, coffee shops, restaurants, bars and, of course, veterinary clinics. It's now a community where people now want to live, not run away from.

We are certainly proud of our role in this story. Dr. Mann illustrates a method that worked. If you get all the foundation pieces and values right, the rest is a lot of work but it will fall into place. Dr. Mann and myself wish you the best of luck.

Brian Faulk, Senior Lender

Introduction

I am a veterinarian and, while I deeply love what I do, I never thought I would be a business owner. Every path, yours included, will take many different directions. I took them all and made plenty of mistakes. But then I learned.

I discovered Brooklyn just after my internship when I was making $28,000 per year working 12 hours a day and learning all I could. After my internship, I did the classic thing and fell in love with the most wonderful woman ever. We found a brand new development on Fulton Street in Clinton Hill Brooklyn, the first of its kind. The apartments were not too expensive, mostly because the homeless took over the building next door and were pretty obvious about it. Nonetheless, we fell in love with the tree-lined streets and the people who walked them. We called our broker and decided we were going to put in an offer. We were told that we couldn't. We couldn't afford a loan and we couldn't afford the modest apartment. As a matter of fact, we probably couldn't afford any apartment in Brooklyn as we got declined for a 200,000-dollar loan.

When the going gets tough, the tough get going. We wrote a loan proposal for 2 million dollars and bought the building next door! I remember getting sick at the thought of that much debt.

I was working in a good practice in Williamsburg and was content saving lives but I also was frustrated. I felt my medicine and business practices were being undervalued and my career options were limited. I felt stymied at the lack of medical agreement. Like you, I felt I could do and offer more. I felt I needed to create a space that was impressive, relaxing and different than the standard veterinary clinic. I wanted people and animals to think they were in an oasis rather than a clinic. I set about building a world class veterinary clinic not because I wanted to but because I needed to.

The principles on which I built my business are all throughout this book but most important to start are empathetic planning and adaptation. Success in anything isn't about information, it's about knowledge. The former are facts, the latter is the creative understanding of facts that allows you to innovate, adapt and evolve. As a vet, I come face to face with evolution every day. All the animals that are around today have found the way to survive and even thrive by adaptation. Like a business, these species have had to adapt and perhaps none more so than the aardvark. This misunderstood creature is an adaptive miracle, so much so that I have named my model for business success after him. You can build success on the following principles: Adaptation, Activismy, Resilience, Drive, Values, Analysis, Respect and Knowledge. The aardvark's adaptability has allowed it to thrive for 23 million years. The aardvark would make a great CEO.

Some call it the process of gentrification but there is something special about Brooklyn and New York City. New York changes through local people starting businesses, hoping and dreaming. It becomes a great city through dreamers making their mark. If the dreamer is successful and creates something unique and lasting, he or she can engage in business activism and create a new environment that will only add to his or her success. Others will come to their neighborhood, just like Clinton Hill called me, and others after me, to come and make their mark. In this book, you will meet a few who created great businesses and affected positive change.

Tess created a small business because she was value driven, desiring everyone in Clinton Hill to eat sustainably. She called each customer her neighbor. Gary spent many years in the food service industry and used his knowledge to create the first real coffee shop in Clinton Hill, which became a destination for me and many others coming to the neighborhood. Sean created an institution of outdoor events because he loved putting people together and turning passers-by into neighbors. Jessica and Rebecca created a successful independent book store at a time when big and little bookstores were going out of business. They listened to the community by building partnerships and giving back. Listening to their stories, it is clear that the principles of the AARDVARK approach work and transcend the veterinary world. We will look into them and use these principles, along with my stories, animals' stories and big business examples as a basis of a guide for your own business success.

Chris Gardner, the author of *Pursuit of Happiness*, tells a story about how he went from being homeless at 28, living in a bathroom with his infant son, to becoming a Wall Street millionaire. He claims he did it because it was in his spiritual DNA. There was nothing special given to him in his genes except his drive to follow his dreams. The most important aspect of his story is to never let anybody, even yourself, tell you that you can't do something. It is your choice if you accept your lot in life or if you want to change it.

Keep in mind as you read these stories, the most important person is you. You have to tell yourself that you can first. The American dream says you can do or be anything. It doesn't guarantee it will work, but you have the right and obligation to yourself to try.

How did this happen? How can you create an environment that is your dream and where you can live your dreams?

The answer is pretty obvious. It happens slowly at first, then all at once. It happens as you cry with owners over sick animals and you laugh with joy as you save other animals. It happens as you counsel kids leaving high school or excite local preschoolers. It happens as you set up solar panels and start providing holistic products throughout the neighborhood. It happens as you see other dreamers follow your lead and you follow theirs. It's a magical process. Let me tell you about it.

An AARDVARK?

What better animal to demonstrate business principles! If you have never seen an Aardvark, you probably won't believe it's a real animal. Most people think of an anteater but the aardvark is more closely related to an elephant or manatee than an anteater and is one of the earliest hoofed animals! There are so many adaptions that have come from a process of convergent evolution. It almost looks like aardvarks took the best parts of several animals ignoring the extraneous parts.

Early warning rabbit ears allow aardvarks to run away quickly and avoid predators

The large nose is similar to a pig snout so the aardvark can sniff out food from a long way away with more olfactory bulbs than any other mammal!

The hoofs have adapted into hard tough spades to dig

The tail is similar to a club, like a kangaroo and can be used if you get too close!

> The toes are webbed like a duck making this mammal a great swimmer!
>
> The skin resembles a bear's and they are sometimes called the earth bear. Try striking through that hard skin!
>
> Through a process of evolution to find out "what works," the aardvark has been around for 23 million years and is not in any danger of leaving us anytime soon. There is much to learn from an aardvark!

Aardvark is also an acronym that I have used to highlight key business principles.

Adaptation
Activism
Respect
Drive
Values
Analysis
Resources
Knowledge

The brain can only focus on one thing at a time, so when articulating an approach like the AARDVARK method, each component is described individually. However, in practice, the components don't exist in isolation but rather are constantly interacting and influencing each other. As you read the chapters, ask yourself which of the components are evident in the stories and how they interact.

At the back of the book there is a short workbook that encourages you to think about the aardvark principles and how you can adapt them into your own business.

Chapter One:

How to Train a Horse

My father and I were driving north of New York City into Duchess County. I was a young teenager and this is a drive we did almost every day, to ride horses in the beautiful countryside. It was beautiful, but it was also much more affordable for lessons upstate and we loved the rugged, less uptight version of riding. My dad, a now small town advertising entrepreneur with limited hours, loved horses. He had owned several thoroughbreds years ago. He preferred the Irish hunter-jumpers and I had spent a lot of my childhood around them. I always wanted a horse too and my dad was open to the idea but it was a hard thing to find.

I had already looked at several other horses but none of them had passed muster. The conventional wisdom had it that inexperienced owners needed experienced horses. The only way for a wild teenager to learn was to have a slow, relaxed horse that would "slow him down and teach him", they would say. I found out an important lesson: wisdom isn't always conventional. The older horses that were offered to me might have been more mellow and savvy than their younger counterparts but they were also falling apart. More than one hard passed a physical on heavy doses of painkillers, only to be hobbling around when the medications wore off. So I had abandoned convention for a bit and found a horse I loved in a back field.

> *"Imagination is more important than knowledge."*
> *Albert Einstein*

Hawaiian Knight hadn't been able to make the grade as a racehorse and wasn't really for sale. They couldn't "break him" (train him for the saddle) at the stable that was home to many successful racing thoroughbreds. He was stubborn and was determined to do his own thing in his own time. He just wouldn't be held down. So he was let to live in a backyard for a bit while they figured out the next step. I worked around the stable for reduced priced lessons so I saw him in the field beyond the barn. I went out to the field to take a good look.

As I strode onto the field he was about 100 yards away from me. For a moment we stood there, sizing each other up. He was 18 months old, which made us both teenagers. A teenage boy and a teenage horse with more than a little in common.

He started to run towards me, breaking into an impressive gallop. I stood my ground mostly in shock. It's an experience being charged at by a horse and I don't entirely recommend it. He kept coming hard and fast, heading straight for me. He kept his line; was this a game of chicken? On he came, closer and closer. I stood still.

When he was almost on me he swerved to my right and then stopped behind me. He reared and whinnied, about as close to a laugh as you can get in a horse. He was looking at me and I swear he was smiling. He came up to me and nudged me with his head a few times. Here was the renegade, the horse that wouldn't be broken, wild and free, a loner with an adventurous spirit.
This was the horse for me.

How does a horse who doesn't know a thing teach a young boy who thinks, like every teenager, he knows everything? How can you go from a non-winnable situation to opening and managing one of the most successful practices in Brooklyn?

I told my dad that this was the horse I wanted and he started the negotiations with the owner's representatives over the phone. A thoroughbred transaction typically takes place in an expensive attorney's office in the heart of the business district, very close to a major financial institution. We were sitting in a Denny's restaurant when this deal was finalized. I was so excited! It was one of the magical moments of my youth, so much so, that when I am in the area I often stop into that very establishment and savor the memories.

There was one thing about my horse I didn't like -- his name. I didn't see him as Hawaiian and wasn't sure he was really a knight. I racked my brain for a good name for him and then when I couldn't find anything I liked I resorted to some teenage irony and settled on John Doe. However when he was registered his name was misspelled and he became John Dough.

Doughboy and I became best friends, which was good because neither of us had any. Well, that's not true exactly. I had a couple of solid friends but otherwise I was something of an outsider. I wasn't unpopular but I was reserved. When my peers were playing baseball and football I was riding horses or playing the cello. I had my moments, though. I was somehow the last man standing for our team in a serious game of Dodgeball. I miraculously managed to evade a slew of balls thrown at me and then I actually caught one. The catch restored our team to full strength and I got a lot of respect. It felt good. However, I continued to do my own thing in my own way -- a lot like Doughboy.

Doughboy and I were getting along well but there was one drawback to owning a spirited, independent horse. If the professionals at the thoroughbred stable couldn't break him how was this 14 year-old going to break him in? How was I going to train him?

How do we train others? How can we teach people and make them more productive? How can we make people want to learn?

My own training at school had been mixed. I excelled at math and science and did well in other subjects like English. My experience of my trainers was also varied. I remember about this time I had an English class assignment. We had to write an essay that finished the sentence, Now that springtime is here *I can finally*....

I really embraced the assignment. I created a whole saga about going to the planet Voltar. I created imaginary characters and fantasy plots. I devised new cities and novel phenomena. It consumed me and I ended up handing in a 20-page story that was part screenplay treatment and part essay. It was a feat of imagination. I had really exercised my creativity and I was anxious to see how well the teacher liked it.

The teacher didn't like it at all. He scoffed at it, gave me a C and said I hadn't answered the question. He railed about the problems, criticizing it mercilessly and did not acknowledge one positive feature, not even the effort. I guess he could not see beyond his own expectations. I was crushed and disappointed that my immense effort was not appreciated. I felt stupid mainly because I obviously was so wrong about my own evaluation of my work. It created doubt as well as shame. I was discouraged. What had I learned? Don't do anything but the minimum for that guy.

Conversely, I had worked hard on a book review for another teacher. I really liked and admired, Dr. Dicker. So when he gave us an assignment to review a classical work I worked really hard to do the best job I could even though I wasn't terribly interested in the subject. Honestly, I was doing it because of Dr. Dicker. I was doing it for Dr. Dicker. I asked friends for feedback and even some editing help and kept working at it until I felt it was the best it could be. Dr. Dicker was pleased with my effort and was so impressed he read my entire paper out to the class. I was ecstatic, vindicated, encouraged and eager to do more -- especially for Dr. D.

Back at the barn I knew that the traditional approach to "training," which involved tying the horse in ropes and asserting one's dominance wasn't going to work with Doughboy. Neither did I really want to do that to him. I had to come up with something different.

My plan was simply to play with him. Specifically, to play so much with him that I would exhaust him and then he would be less resistant to my efforts at training. We ran around until he was fatigued and then I "broke" him, to use the parlance of the day. I hope that I didn't "break" him but rather got him to go along with his training. I'd like to think he saw me as his version of Dr Dicker. Happily, those older methods of "breaking" have given way to more enlightened techniques that are more like what I was able to do with Doughboy.

Doughboy and I had some wonderful times. We laughed a lot together. I found out that Doughboy loved not only carrots but dingdongs and Bucsh beer. He was continually low brow. I had pestered my dad for a cat forever but when that wasn't working I switched my request to a dog and miraculously, one was soon a member of the household. He was a black Labrador called Jet and he and Doughboy loved playing together. Doughboy would put his nose on Jet's back and the dog took off -- with Doughboy holding his head on the top of Jet's tail. It was a hilarious sight made even better by the obvious joy they were having playing together.

Doughboy did eventually find an equine friend. Oreo was a horse in the same stable, owned by a very beautiful pair of twin girls about my age. Oreo and Doughboy struck up quite a relationship, which is more than I could do with either of the twins. And one day Doughboy taught me a lesson, my first lesson in veterinary medicine.

Oreo was acting a little strangely and for some reason wanted to roll around on the ground, but Doughboy was being atypically aggressive. He was kicking and striking out at Oreo. I couldn't work out what was happening. Then it occurred to me that Doughboy didn't want Oreo to be rolling around on the ground. He was preventing his friend from doing this. Why?

I had been around horses long enough to know that colic can be fatal to a horse. The equine GI system can be fragile and colic can be a major problem, especially if the horse starts rolling around on the ground, potentially tying up his intestines.

I figured out that Oreo had colic and that Doughboy was trying to prevent him from making the situation worse. Doughboy was kicking and biting at Oreo to keep him up. At least that's what I thought. Was this an accurate diagnosis or a figment of my creative teenage imagination? Just to be sure, I called the vet immediately. Sure enough, Oreo had colic. It was my first big animal rescue. Well, I can't take all the credit -- my buddy Doughboy had a big part to play as well.

Doughboy taught me more than just about colic. He taught me it was okay to be independent and unconventional -- more than okay. He taught me that force was not a very effective way of training any animal. He also taught me that constraints aren't meant to hold you down, they're meant to fire you up.

I didn't articulate it at the time but Doughboy taught me two important lessons that gave this boy a chance to earn some serious dough, independence and engagement.

For one thing, he showed me that it was not just okay but critically important to be independent. Independence gives you the opportunity to separate yourself from the crowd. This allows you not to fall foul of the easy and natural tendency to accept the status quo, to think along with everyone else. There's no competitive advantage in being part of the crowd.

> "The essence of an independent mind lies not in what it thinks, but how it thinks."
>
> Christopher Hitchens.

An independent mindset allows you to think differently and, therefore, innovate. It allows you to consider everything from a fresh perspective, which can make a huge difference in a business. Just making one system or process more efficient can be the difference between success and failure. An independent mindset is an innovative mindset and it has enabled me to achieve success and do things that I would not have been able to do if I had not learned to question everything.

> "The third-rate mind is only happy when it is thinking with the majority. The second-rate mind is only happy when it is thinking with the minority. The first-rate mind is only happy when it is thinking."
>
> A.A. Milne

The second lesson that Doughboy and Dr. Dicker taught me was about engagement, currently a hot topic in business. **How do you get the most out of your team, whether they are partners or employees?**

The old command and control management style has outlived its usefulness. Even Doughboy would not be forced into compliance. Employees at whatever level might do a task if it is part of their job description but how do you get them to really *own* it? There's a big difference between going through the motions of getting a job done and being fully engaged. There is a lot of evidence from numerous large scale studies that companies with highly engaged employees are far more innovative and successful on any number of measures. For example, in one large scale study, 67% of highly engaged employees recommended their company's products and services to others compared to only 3% of low engaged workers.

> "When people are financially invested they want a return. When people are emotionally invested, they want to contribute."
>
> *Simon Sinek*

Engagement is built on trust and respect. That's how I got Doughboy trained -- I played with him enough until he trusted me. We also respected each other to know that we wouldn't intentionally harm each other -- on the contrary we would have each other's back. Engagement is built around an authentic relationship in which each party honors and values the other. That means including people in decisions, asking their opinions, valuing their input and effort -- just like Dr. D did with me. When you create that ethic and reinforce it, team members will want to do everything they can to make the team succeed. You will have turned a job into a passion and an employee into a collaborator.

> "The only way to do great work is to love what you do."
>
> Steve Jobs

Stories from the Wild Horses

Like many other animals, horses react to the emotions of the people and animals around them. My reluctance to "break" doughboy using the typical training procedures lead to a great bond between us. Here's a piece that summarizes the empathy of horses.

Equine Empathy
"Horses are naturally and always empathetic. The members of the herd feel what is going on for the other members of the herd. This is why the horses often move as one unit when in the herd. Empathetic responses help the animals to become bonded, develop trust, respect and create loyalties. A relationship that has involved empathy will be deeper and more compelling than one that has not. If we have empathetic relationships with our horses they truly become our trusted companions and we become that to them as well. If this sort of relationship is established, generally the horse will really try as hard as it can to comply with the wishes of the human. This is partly because the human has stepped up as the empathetic great leader for the horse. That person has become the great leader of the herd."

Franklin Levinson's Way of the Horse at
http://www.wayofthehorse.org/Essays/empathetic-horseman.html

Chapter Two

College, Cuba and Creativity: Adaptation

When I was a kid I wanted to be a smokejumper. Those are guys who jump out of choppers and planes into wildfires. My back-up plan was to be in the Coast Guard and jump out of planes and choppers and rescue people from treacherous situations. Now I had successfully navigated high school it was time to jump into college. I still wasn't sure what I wanted to do, except explore my options.

One option I never considered was not going to college . There was no question that I was going immediately after high school. I think now that there's a growing acceptance of the notions that college is not for everyone, that taking time off to other things might be useful and that there are other ways of developing as a young adult. But more than a decade ago those ideas weren't really even discussed and the fact is that I was really looking forward to my college experience. So my choice was where to go to school not whether I should go to school.

I applied to nine schools before I even set foot on a campus. The first school I visited was Bates College in Lewiston, Maine. It is a highly rated liberal arts college, routinely being rated among the nation's top 25 in that category. The College was actually founded by abolitionists and some of the first students were freed slaves. The school was one of the first to adopt an optional SAT policy. Applicants did not have to submit SAT or other standardized test scores. In fact, after nearly three decades of this policy, the college has shown that there is no significant difference in graduation rates between those who submitted formalized scores on their applications and those who did not.

As you might imagine for an institution that was liberal, artsy and a college, there was a fair degree of partying going on after school hours. My overnight stay was a lot of fun. Bates, while now a non-sectarian school, was at one time a Baptist college. Perhaps that's why students were being given $45 tickets for being under the influence of alcohol! I found out that a hundred such tickets had been given out and it was just the beginning of the academic year. I had a blast there but I didn't think the college was right for me. The search continued.

I next visited Colby College in Waterville, Maine. It, too, was a very well respected liberal arts college. In fact, it was the 12th oldest independent liberal arts college in the country and the first all-male school in New England to accept female students, which it did in 1871. It also had a lot of overseas students and emphasis on studying abroad which was a big draw for me. Again, I had a good time there but it too didn't quite feel right. I was definitely working on gut instinct as to which school to choose. Many of the schools were of excellent quality and offered similar opportunities. I just thought I would know the right school when I saw it, or more accurately, felt it. Rationally, any of the schools would be a good choice, I just wanted it to feel right.

> "I must be willing to give up what I am in order to become what I will be."
>
> Albert Einstein

I next went to visit another school that was somewhat similar to Bates and Colby. Hampshire College in Amherst, Massachusetts didn't have the pedigree of Bates or Colby. It was relatively new, having been started in 1970 as an educational experiment. It has an alternative curriculum, emphasizes portfolios of student work rather than test scores and eschews grades and exams for professor's narratives about students' abilities and achievements. More than half of the alumni go on to get a Master's degree and it ranks in the top 30 U.S. College for percentages of alumni who proceed to get doctorates.

I loved the atmosphere at Hampshire! I knew it was for right me almost immediately. I knew that I would get a real education, in the sense that I would learn how to really explore a subject, not just learn facts. I would learn how to really think rather than simply memorize. I would be challenged rather than merely tested. I passionately believe in this model of education. For me education is about learning to think critically, learning how to explore a subject, learning to think not just outside the box but without a box at all. Interestingly, the evolution of higher education at least, is heading in this direction. Several major schools have proposed, or already have in place, courses in which factual material is learned online at home and that the class is the place where creative, innovative discussion and implementation of ideas takes place. Amen!

When I first arrived at Hampshire, I had talked with my college advisor/mentor and he asked me what I wanted to do. I was a bit stumped, to be honest. However, because of my love of animals, the notion of being a vet appealed to me. So when put on the spot, I admitted to my advisor that Veterinary medicine was something that I was interested in.

My advisor didn't have to do much research to tell me that if I wanted to go down the vet path, I would have to take courses in subjects like algebra, physics and chemistry. No! Every cell in my body rebelled. Those subjects were SO boring! I didn't come to college to be bored, I came to explore. I gave up on the vet idea and elected for a mix of social science, earth science and arts courses. My first class was a geology class where we studied sand dunes and swamps. I loved a sociology class about neighborhoods and another in political geography. I found the classes stimulating, the discussions enlightening and the lack of tests, exams and grades, a relief.

I loved Hampshire and it was absolutely the right choice for me. Hampshire was not chosen because of any of the academic accolades or research opportunities or even because they don't have tests or grades and have a different theory of education. It was chosen because it felt right. Hampshire was a joy because of the constant exploration. Without tests or grades, the only thing the professors could really do was to inspire creativity and innovative projects so they had something to talk about. Instead of striving to become an A+ student, all of us wanted to become unique students who were given the freedom to truly explore a topic. The freedom created by not having tests and grades gave students the time and the incentive to immerse themselves in a topic.

At Hampshire, I also got the opportunity to study abroad. So while my fellow students went off to Europe and South America, I, of course, wanted to do something totally out of the box. I went to Cuba. as part of the first program where American kids would be studying with Cuban kids in a Cuban University. There would be five of us.

Part of me wanted to go there because, well, hardly anyone from the US studies abroad there. I was looking for unique opportunities. Cuba was forbidden fruit and I knew nothing about it, not even the language. This caused some practical problems. In some ways I was not equipped to go at all, especially because I was in classes with Cuban students and my Cuban Spanish wasn't that great. For example, my gringo butt was kicked in an environmental economics class. The professor kept using the term *Medio Ambiente*. I knew at that point that ambiente meant the environment, like ambience, and medio meant middle or half (or so I thought). So I raised my hand and asked the professor why he kept talking about half the environment. Instead of the professor saying I was an idiot and that *medio ambiente* meant the outside environment and *ambiente* meant the inside environment, he stopped and pronounced me a genius. He said he never thought about it and wow, in an environmental economics class it's amazing how we don't consider the outside, half of the inside. Communication worked well, even if was never intentional.

I hooked up with a climbing group. I loved the group because we would go out to some really remote places and climb -- and then get stuck there. We would need a ride back into Camaguey, the third largest city in Cuba. We would sometimes wait on these dusty roads for hours. Unlike New York where you don't look at anybody when waiting at a bus stop and now mercifully have cell phones to stare at, waiting in Cuba, especially on a remote road is different. You sing. And Dance. We would just sing and dance for hours while waiting for a ride from truckers or farmers. I liked that more than the climbing part.

My final thesis for my study abroad was entitled *Un Parque Sin Cercas: A park without fences*. It reflected the fact that Cuba had reforested more land since 1950, it's major regime change, a feat not achieved by any other country. They did it because the Cubans don't wall off parks like we do. Instead of separating the park -- creating a distinction between the park and living space -- people live within the park and create sustainable use areas, which in turn allows for thoughtful and appropriate land development and use. I studied this in an area called the Seirra de Cubitas (or little Cuban mountains). It was a great example of creative thinking and innovation benefitting everyone and not creating boxes.

Another example of creative adaptation by the Cubans resulted from the collapse of the Soviet Union on whom Cuba had depended. The break-up of the Soviet federation created a period of austerity in Cuba and the locals had to adapt to what Cuban's called "the special period". For example, there was a severe shortage of fertilizer. To adapt, people teamed together to create earthworm farms, which solved the problem as the worms would fertilizer the soil better than some petroleum fertilizer without all the nasty environmental side effects. I was inspired watching this creative collaboration. Overall, I had a wonderful and valuable six months in Cuba.

When I was back at Hampshire enjoying socializing with my dorm mates. I felt more comfortable talking with others and I really developed my social skills, as I guess most people do during their college years. All the dorms were connected and I would just walk from hall to hall and if a door was open, it was fair game to talk to anyone who was there. I always had my door open, especially when I wasn't there, so friends could just hang out in my room. I remember people used to walk by, excited that it was raining so they could go out in old clothes and stomp in puddles. And stomping in the rain featured in one particularly memorable day in my college career.

Nearby Hampshire, there was the Cook Family Farm, which had been a dairy farm for generations. They were the sweetest people you could ever meet. The dairy farm was declining and several dairy farmers were selling their land off to developers as more people wanted to live in the pioneer valley instead of farming in it. People, including prominent professors, were saying that small scale farming had outlived its usefulness and that by buying small scale, you were just perpetuating a lifestyle, not a functional system.

The Cooks had some cows which, of course, pooped. At the time, we were worried about excess nitrogen in the water, leading to algae blooms and excessive waste in the water making people sick. The Cooks were smart as well as sweet. They also knew that nitrogen and cow poop was a great fertilizer. Instead of doing what every other farmer did -- put the cow poop on the side of the farm, usually near a stream -- they put the poop in the center of the farm so when it rained, the nutrients would travel from the fecal pile through the farm.

On my 19th birthday, I went to the farm with some friends for a science class. Because it was my birthday, I was elected to catch rain water from the top of the fecal pile while my friends collected rain water from the sides of the farm in an attempt to compare nitrogen levels. The idea was that we would take the samples back to the lab at Hampshire and measure them with a mass spectrometer to see if this was helping the Cooks use less fertilizer and thus lessening the hazard to the drinking water.

It was a cold day in April so the fecal pile was solid. I remember climbing to the top, which must have been like 100 feet! Okay, more like 7 feet but it felt high! I got my fresh samples and then I exaggeratedly jumped off the pile to show off to my friends (well, it was my birthday). Pride comes before a fall. The semi-solid fecal piles were not as stable as I thought. I fell in waist high. While my friends were rolling on the ground laughing uncontrollably, I ran as fast as I could to the stream and tried to wash off in the frigid waters. It didn't help, much. Let's just say, that I remained unattached despite having a great birthday party that night! And I smelled for the entire week.

In following their ideals and adopting to new environments, the Cooks have since celebrated their favorite cow, Flayor, and created a wonderful local ice cream and food stand. If you are ever in Hadley Massachussetts, please do look them up and have some incredible raw local ice cream! Adding in a small dairy to their dairy farm was a great success and example of a company that can adapt to changing times.

I was privileged to have had a wonderful college experience. I learned how to think critically. I learned how to think creatively. I learned to have no fear in exploring new ideas and to try different experiences. I met lots of interesting people. It was the ideal preparation for life even if it didn't specifically lead me down a career path. Career wise I was actually off the beaten path. I wasn't sure what I was going to do next. But I was prepared for whatever was next, being an auto mechanic, a scuba diver, and a wall street project manager.

Stories from the Wild: Cows and Intelligence

Every animal has a particular skill and purpose, even -- or perhaps especially -- those animals that most people think of as merely reflexive organism with little or no intelligence. No life form should be underestimated. Here's a nice piece from the Huffington Post about cows.

"Alexandra Green, a 21-year-old student at the University of Sydney, developed a test that provides evidence of cows' sophisticated cognitive abilities. Green found that dairy cows could follow sound through a maze in order to find food, suggesting heightened executive function and decision-making abilities. "

"These capabilities shouldn't be surprising to us, says zoologist Dr. Daniel Weary, a professor in the Animal Welfare Program at the University of British Columbia.
'These are highly developed mammals that have been solving

problems for a long, long time,' he told The Huffington Post. 'If anything, it reflects poorly on us that we're surprised that these animals are smart. Of course these animals are smart.'"

"For the experiment, Green trained six dairy cows to navigate a large T-shaped maze modeled after smaller mazes used on mice and rats. The cows were trained to follow sound through the maze in order to get to their food. "

"Four out of the six heifers nailed the test, while the other two scored 75 percent. One cow was able to find the food in under 20 seconds on the first day of learning the maze, suggesting intelligence levels can vary widely between animals.

'They would turn their heads to where the sound was,' Green told New Zealand Farmer. 'They would really think about it, whereas in the beginning they were making a guess.'"

From the Huffington Post at http://www.huffingtonpost.com/entry/cows-are-way-smarter-than-you-thought_55b631e-de4b0224d8832b382

Chapter Three

In Search of a Vocation

When I was at Hampshire, I changed my major all the time. This was easy to do as there were no tests or grades and lots of ideas. So, like many other students, I changed my major to whatever happened to stimulate my interest at the time. The entire curriculum was focused on inspiring independent projects, so there were many opportunities to go off and explore fun things with a view to possibly pursuing them further, and perhaps even developing a career.

As I mentioned in the first chapter, individual teachers inspire learning and I had a great geology teacher at Hampshire. He made earth sciences so interesting that I made it a major -- for a while. He would make the rocks tell great stories and we did an amazing project on the sand dunes on Cape Cod. But when he wasn't around the rocks bored me. I then shifted my attention to natural disasters; it seemed like a very cool topic. I studied volcanoes and other fascinating stuff but then it occurred to me that volcanologists weren't a terribly exciting crowd -- it just didn't get my lava going. I also studied social justice and along with the environmental sciences, with some agriculture and animal science, graduated with a sort of geology/social justice/environmental science/agriculture major. Not the most transferable major.

> "Education is an admirable thing but it is worth noting from time to time that nothing worth knowing can be taught."
>
> Oscar Wilde

It will probably come as no surprise to you that I really wasn't ready to pursue a career or any further education after graduating from Hampshire. I was excited to simply continue to do what I was inspired to do. Like most of the current graduates, I didn't give much thought to the postgraduate lifestyle. I wanted to be interesting and to do that I had be interested. I had a passion for a lot of things and was willing to follow where my interests led me. Whatever I did I wanted to do it with passion.

> "Education is not the filling of a pail but the lighting of a fire."
>
> William Butler Yeats

Initially, my passion led me to the garage. I was an auto mechanic for a while, which I loved, In fact, fixing cars taught me a lot about surgical techniques and I liked being dirty. I knew that wouldn't be my ultimate vocation and besides there aren't that many cars in New York City.

I thought long and hard about my next career move and decided that I had a passion for scuba diving. Without being qualified as a certified instructor, I learned everything I could and sold equipment, taught others and did research for the national science foundation. But when that project dried up I determined that my future didn't lay in Scuba either. It was time to come up for air. However, I did learn some physiology while in this field that was helpful later in my career. I also continually learned that education is a great way to inspire people.

At this point the dotcom business was really taking off and I thought that being able to afford dinner might be a good idea. I had several friends who were doing well in the burgeoning hi-tech industry. They encouraged me to join them even though I didn't have much formal hi-tech education. When I mentioned to my friends that I had no formal qualifications their responses were "You can program a VCR can't you?" It was a great time.

They encouraged me to create my own company, give myself a grand title as a Project Manager and start knocking on doors, virtually rather than literally. So I created NulSum Studios (Nul set actually means "zero" in geek talk) and went live with my company and website. An hour later I got my first gig.

The gig was to create some content, specifically a style guide, for a large financial website. They asked me whether I could create such a style guide and I said, "no problem but you need something more advanced, more time is needed," even though I had no idea what a 'style guide' actually was. They wanted it in a week but I said that a really good style guide would take four weeks. The extra time gave me the opportunity to consult with my more informed buddies about what I needed to do, or really just find out what a style guide was I did produce the style guide -- and promptly got a lot of compliments on it thanks to my friends' support. I was now an experienced hi-tech consultant!

I come from a long line of entrepreneur risk takers. My grandfather claimed he could do anything and basically faked it until he made it. My dad was a journalist who turned himself into a major media and advertising consulting company that occupied two floors of the Chrysler building in Manhattan. Then he gave it up when he wanted to be with his kids and live a simpler life. Style guides wouldn't have phased them either. It has nothing to do with genetics, but rather with the willingness to try!

It was a great time to be in the internet business and my reputation grew. In fact, it grew so much that Morgan Stanley recruited me to run a very exciting project. I was actually hired to develop and run their media streaming division using flash technology. That might seem almost mundane now but at the dawn of the new millennium, this was futuristic stuff. Of course, I didn't know anything about flash technology either, but I knew it wouldn't take me long to learn.

I was very excited about this incredible opportunity. It was a huge step up with a major company. I was slated to start in March, 2001 and I was psyched. However, a week before the scheduled start, Morgan Stanley called me to say that the whole project was cancelled. They were very apologetic and actually offered me a severance package, which softened the blow.

This disappointing episode brought me face-to-face with a burning career question: **How much control did I want over my career?** In the internet world I had seen people and businesses being bought and sold with regularity, some making fortunes, some losing opportunities. But the thought of not being in control of my destiny was troubling. It was time for something new.

> *"There is no passion in life in playing small -- for settling for the life that is less than the one you are capable of living."*
>
> *Nelson Mandela*

I decided that perhaps it was now time to go to veterinary school. So, I took a job at the Brooklyn Zoo. Erin was the head tech and she needed help! There was so much to do. There was a difference between the vets and the zookeepers. The zookeepers were much less hands-on while the vets were more like doctors. As a tech/zookeeper I enjoyed the distinction. This wasn't some internship in a comfortable veterinary practice giving shots and vaccines, this was real contact with animals, with the emphasis on the animals and the politics of differing viewpoints.

Erin was terrific and taught me a lot about organization. Each morning we would create a 'to do' list and work our way steadily through it all day. This was extremely valuable experience and a necessary skill for this free spirit. I was able to repay Erin a little later for the opportunity and her valuable education while she was able to help out at the Brooklyn clinic.

> "To Know that one life has breathed easier because you have lived. This is to have succeeded."
>
> Ralph Waldo Emerson

Working at the Brooklyn Zoo brought me into contact with a variety of characters. For one thing, the zoo was the receiving center for animals coming from abroad and needing to be quarantined, so all sorts of interesting creatures graced our clinic.

Harry Houdini was an aardvark who simply wouldn't stay in his enclosure. He could escape from anywhere and I would find him in all sorts of places, like in the catbox, under coats, dark places -- anywhere. He was a teenager and acted like one. He would wake up very slowly and take his time before he moved anywhere. He loved mealworms and when I held one in my hand to get him moving, Harry would lazily lift his snout and then extend his spaghetti-like tongue, weaving it through my fingers to get to the mealworm.

Another memorable lesson involved five baboons. There were two males and three female baboons. One of the baboons, Bole, was attached to two of the females and the other baboon, Simen, was attached to the other female. It was a stable arrangement -- until Simen got sick and was removed from the group. Bole wasted no time to claim Simen's Girl. Simen recovered and within a week was ready to go back to the troupe. But how would this affect the sexual dynamics of the group?

We decided to separate the males and the females, and then when the time was right we re-introduced Bole and Simen. Instantly, both went to all of the females, each trying to claim them all for himself. There was a short period of sexual chaos and then the females took matters into their own hands. They separated themselves and each went in different directions, neutralizing the boys' efforts to dominate them. It was as if the females were telling the guys how it was going to be and there was nothing they could do about it! It's clear that the girls had had enough and wanted some peace and quiet.

I was working at the zoo, rather than in The World Trade Center, Tower Two for Morgan Stanley, on 9/11. I was taking classes on Mondays and Wednesdays at Pace University right near the Twin Towers but this was a Tuesday and so I took the Q train from southern Brooklyn to the zoo. I was going about my morning routines when someone came into the clinic and said that a plane had hit the towers. Before long there was no cell phone reception and then smoke filled the sky. One aspect of that disaster that many people will remember is the enormous amount of paper that started falling from the sky. The paper was the fall-out from every office that had been destroyed. It was like a gruesome ticker tape parade -- but this was no parade. We had to secure the zoo, which meant I spent a lot of time chasing down the baboons and closing enclosures, and then, once we made sure that all the animals were safe, I walked home in a daze.

As well as learning about organization, I also learned about resourcefulness while working with Erin at the zoo. We were always adapting and creating innovative solutions. For example, the rabbits were prone to breaking their backs and, to aid their recovery, we built small skateboards and transformed them into bunny wheelchairs to support them through their recovery.

Working at the zoo was a wonderful experience. I learned a lot about animals -- and humans. I learned a lot about organization and productivity. And I also learned about adaptation and innovation. It also helped me determine my career path. I was sure I wanted to be a vet.

Due to entry requirements, I could only apply to two veterinary schools. I also knew full well that vet school is very competitive, and harder to get into than medical school. My best chance was Cornell, which took a disproportionate number of students from New York. I had an interesting resume, was more mature (i.e. older) than the typical applicant and felt sure I was a good candidate. Going to my interview, I felt confident that I was going to be selected. The person who "interviewed me was blunt. Because I had gone to Hampshire and had no grades or test scores there was no way for them to evaluate me. Sorry, no veterinary school for you, and please help yourself to tissues on the way out.

I was devastated. My plan B was to go to a veterinary school in the Caribbean but my mother in particular insisted I keep trying schools in the US even though the competition was fierce, especially for someone without a college GPA.

I had also applied to the Ivy League option, the University of Pennsylvania, and I got accepted. The Caribbean was looking particularly appealing. I mean, Penn would be ultra-competitive and there would be things like tests and exams; I took a deep hard breath.

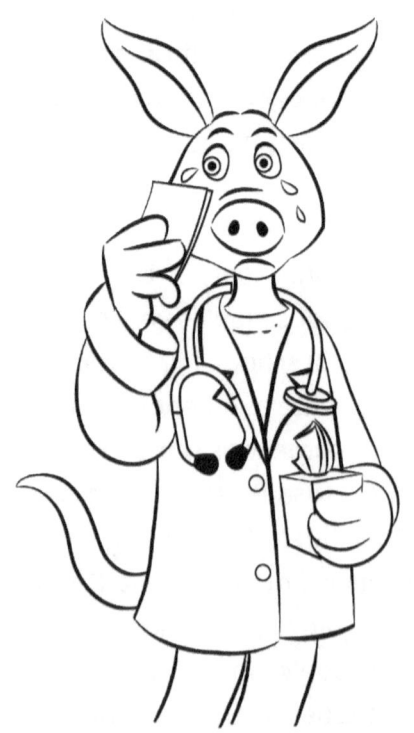

Of course, I accepted Penn's offer. The first semester was the hardest. I had to take a course in biochemistry, which was notoriously hard. While taking that course I was ever mindful that if you fail a class at the Vet school at Penn, you're out of the school. No pressure..

Our first final was biochemistry, a notoriously hard class for those who majored in biochemistry, not just me. Everyone was a little apprehensive, even those with an IQ of 150. I took it and figured it was touch and go whether I had passed. I didn't want to go to get the results, which were posted by the afternoon. I waited until night time when I thought no one else would be there and snuck back into the department.

I was sweating as I reached for the note that would determine my future. Passing was a 70. I waited, summoned up my courage and then looked at my score. It was 72! I was ecstatic and broke into a huge smile. It was then that I heard the sound of crying coming from under the staircase. I went over to explore and found Christine, a fellow student with an IQ of about 150, crying. She surely hadn't failed? No, she hadn't. She was in tears because it was the first time in her life that she had got less than an A. She got an 89 and was devastated.

The rest of the program was relatively easy. Time flew by and before I knew it I was a newly minted Vet doing a final internship. Years of studying had led up to this moment. I was excited if a little apprehensive.

I had qualified in all the book knowledge I needed and it was now time to venture out into the world and get real experience. On this rotation at Vet school I found myself on the large animal surgical unit. As an intern it was my job to assess the animal and interview the owner to find out the nature of the problem. Then I would report back to the surgeon with enough detail so that he or she would know exactly what was happening and could then devise the plan of treatment.

My big day arrived. I was ready and my first client had been checked in and was waiting in one of the smaller, padded stalls. As I entered I could see that my patient was a beautiful Gazelle. He was a Tompkins Gazelle, a slightly smaller species from Africa with amazing twisted horns. For protection, the horns were covered with PVC piping. The Gazelle wandered up to me and nudged me lovingly a few times.

I turned my attention to the owners, two elderly gentlemen.

"What can I do for you?" I asked.

"We need our reindeer neutered," one of them said.

Reindeer? That was not promising. I was fascinated and intrigued by how these two guys ended up with an African gazelle.

"We wanted to get married," said one of the men. I assumed he meant that they wanted to marry each other. Back in 2005 that would certainly be a problem in the US.

"So we went to get married in Africa. And while we there, we saw this animal and decided it was a great symbol of our love. So, as a sort of mutual wedding present, we bought it and shipped it home," said the other man.

Okay, but a little strange. But why did they want the gazelle neutered? The answer wasn't long in coming.

"Because it's a symbol of our love, we sometimes shower with it. And recently it has been getting more and more amorous with us in the shower," the man continued with a perfectly straight face.

Up to this point in my life, when I thought of the word 'mounted' with horned animals I always imagined a massive antlered head on a wall. This discussion was conjuring up different, if somewhat unsettling, associations and images. This is also around the time that I noticed that those large antlers where covered in foam piper fitters for everyone's protection.

"I'm not sure neutering him will make him that much less amorous," I suggested.

The men weren't having any of that.

"We have already bought three sets of neuticles," the other partner added with enthusiasm.

Neuticles are fake testicles that are designed to imitate the natural ones. They are typically made of silicone and one of their purposes is to alleviate an animal's purported stress and depression at losing the real things. The Creator, Gregg Miller was awarded the Ig Nobel Prize -- a parody of the real thing -- a bit like neuticles.

So my first question that I had to answer as a vet was this.

"Which of these pairs of neuticles should we have put in our baby?"

The men proceeded to show me the three pairs of fake balls they had acquired. They explained that they had bought one pair that was smaller than the existing equipment, one pair about the same size and another pair larger than what the Gazelle was currently carrying. They wanted to cover all eventualities.

"Which do you think we should have implanted, Doc?'" pressed one of the men.

I often tell this story and ask people what they would have done. Would they have given into the larger than normal size and thus satisfy some desire for "big balls?" Would they have said the normal size to replace what was already there? Would they have chosen smaller than normal neuticels knowing that the scrotum may undergo shrinkage and the smaller balls would be less stress? Nobody I asked really had the same response I did, probably because the story is a bit out of the norm.

This might have been my first official professional consultation but I was sure this idea was mildly insane, and more importantly, not in the best interests of the animal. The grounds for wanting the gazelle neutered in the first place -- the owners' desire for a peaceful shower -- could have easily been accommodated by arranging for separate bathing facilities for the gazelle and not showering with the animal. Second, I wasn't convinced that neutering the animal would necessarily change his shower time behavior. Third, I didn't think that the neuticles would assuage the gazelle's depression and shame -- if indeed he felt those two emotions. Fourth, I don't like any form of cosmetic surgery.

"I don't think you should have any of them implanted," I said with authority.

The men looked a bit peeved.

"It's not a good reason to neuter him. And frankly, he'll be happier without the fakes. It's nice that you were thoughtful enough to buy the expensive silicone ones but I honestly can't recommend that procedure at all," I said defiantly.

The men weren't happy.

I told then I would discuss the situation with the surgeon who would make the ultimate decision.

I'm not sure that the surgeon completely believed me when I briefed him on the situation but a few moments with the patient and his owners convinced him I wasn't pulling his leg. While he was impressed by the quality of the fake testicles, he agreed with my opinion and together we stood firm.

The gazelle maintained his masculinity. I have no idea what happened to the neuticles.

My vet career was on its way.

Stories from the Wild:
Empathic Gorillias

Frans DeWaal is a primatologist and author who writes engagingly about animal behavior. His writing strongly suggests that empathy is widespread in the animal kingdom. He writes:

"The possibility that empathy resides in parts of the brain so ancient that we share them with rats should give pause to anyone comparing politicians with those poor, underestimated creatures."

In one of De Waal's stories, empathy and respect is clearly evident.

There was a gorilla who found a bird flapping its wings on the ground, clearly injured trying to fly but failing. The Gorilla picked up the bird in its large hands, extended them and let the bird go. The bird flew for a second before falling back down to earth. The Gorilla picked up the bird and set off for the nearest tall tree. He climbed to the top of the tree, carefully protecting the bird as he did. When her reached the top of the tree he let the bird, go and with enough air beneath its wings, it flew again.

Chapter Four

Starting a business:
Organizing, Operationalizing and Emphatic Planning

After graduating from vet school I found a job working with a husband and wife team that ran a veterinary clinic in Williamsburg, Brooklyn. They had a solid reputation and ran a conventional practice by which I mean that they were into holistic and alternative approaches on paper but provided adequate care along with a lot of vaccines and dog food. They preferred easy answers and simple puppy cases over comprehensive medical solutions.

It was a good apprenticeship for me but, before long, I realized that I had a different treatment philosophy. When I realized I was spearheading their medicine, I started considering my next move. When my employers found out I was considering opening my own practice they fired me, fearful that I might take some of their clients with me. Apparently this is pretty typical, although hurtful, in any business environment. It is ironic that both the need for freedom and then the put off by prior employers is a common thread in many start up's that I have interviewed. What happened next certainly surprised me.

> "An organization's ability to learn, and translate that learning into action rapidly, is the ultimate competitive advantage."
>
> Jack Welch

I had found a great apartment for my fiancé Jessie and I on Fulton Street, a part of Brooklyn that was in need of help. We were denied a loan for the apartment so I stepped up my game. I realized that if you are denied for a loan, then maybe you just aren't asking for enough or doing enough analysis! I made a bid for an entire apartment building that sat empty next door thinking, "why not?". I knew I could make it work if I worked smart enough. I thought the site would make for a great vet practice, as well as giving us a living space above the clinic. It would allow me to practice the medicine that I want to practice and have an apartment on top to boot! Having been denied the loan for a $200,000 home I initially got approval for a $2 million building, which included some build-out. The building was owned by a company which had planned to open a physical rehabilitation facility, and in fact there were various pieces of exercise equipment still in the building.

While I was in the process of negotiating this property I set about drawing up a business plan to convince others. My vision was to create a center of excellence, taking a holistic approach that respected my clients and owners. Giving back to the community and caring about all the stakeholders, including clients, staff and neighbors, were also integral parts of the plan.

I was progressing nicely with the business plan when the original bank loan fell through. The major bank had apparently laid off my loan specialist and said that since the loan specialist who wrote the commitment letter was laid off, the commitment letter was invalid. The realtor I was working with at the time questioned me and asked whether I was really up to the challenge, especially as a competitor was going to open up three blocks away. Oh man! It would have been easy to get discouraged and rethink the entire idea. But, yes, I was definitely up for the challenge. Successful entrepreneurs do their research and then double down when they are confident about it. They need it to work and thus they make it work. I went in search of a new lender. I found the perfect fit.

Live Oak is a specialized lender that works specifically with veterinary practices. Brian, my initial contact at Live Oak liked that I had been a bartender previously because it meant I could take to people and empathize. I don't think experience as a bartender is a normal bank check list item! Live Oak couldn't have been a better match. Finding a partner who not only had faith in me and my plan, but knew how to help, made the project that much easier.

The key to my business approach was empathetic planning. This meant that I wanted to design the business with my clients and patients in mind. I wanted them to have the optimum experience and to do that I had to put myself in their shoes -- and paws.

Empathetic planning led to various adaptations and strategies. I have often found the exam rooms in most vet practices to be incredibly small. There's often not enough room for an animal and his owner and the vet and/or a technician. Therefore, I designed the exam rooms to be spacious and comfortable. I wanted the animals to feel safe not cramped. In addition to spacious exam rooms, I eschewed the usual stainless steel examining tables in favor of more welcoming Corian counter tops with yoga mats that made the table cozy for the animals. I didn't want to have fight the animals to stay still, I wanted them to feel safe and comfortable.

I wanted to make the whole clinic welcoming and did everything I could to achieve that effect, which included the aroma of freshly baked bread and other pleasing smells. Even having a zen designer come and help with the flow and colors.

> "In the game of life, less diversity means fewer options for change. Wild or domesticated, panda or pea, adaptation is the requirement for survival."
>
> Cary Fowler

Some of the other innovations involved operational procedures. As well as standard note taking, all the employees were trained in taking meaningful observations. This evolved over time but one of the questions we asked was why the owner gave the pets their names. This made the names much more meaningful and thus memorable as well as providing some insight into the owners and their relationships with their animals. It also helped to create a very personal atmosphere.

On the technology side, I also innovated by investing in an ultrasound machine, which is not standard in most vet practices. As you will read later, this proved to be a critical investment on many occasions.

I selected employees who had good interpersonal skills and a great attitude. Honestly, short of high technology or high science jobs, most people can be taught to do almost anything. Their personality and behavior was critical; skills can always be taught. I made it a point not to hire anyone with veterinary experience because I didn't want anybody's bad habits.

As the clinic evolved, we did have some meetings but there was also a lot of one-on-one time. There really wasn't very much conflict amongst the employees and on the two occasions when two team members seemed to be at odds I successfully resorted to the "lunch tactic." The lunch tactic involved talking briefly to the two employees who were at odds, giving them my credit card so they could have lunch together, and telling them that if they didn't sort it out themselves, one of them would be fired. Sorry, can't say who. This tactic worked very well on both occasions. I also bought the scrubs that all team members required and provided them with everything they needed to do their jobs well. I also provided cross-training so each team member knew everything about the clinic and could, if necessary, step into almost any role. I learned that this was more motivating than money in many cases as people love to learn almost as much as I love to teach.

Some of this was in my business plan, some I learned. A business plan is, of course, just a guide. The real business begins the day you open your doors and then the real planning begins.

On our first day, my five-member team and I were still putting furniture together, putting away medicines, ripping down paper and putting signs in the window. Some of my friends who I had contracted to do some of the build-out were also still there putting the finishing touches to the clinic. The 'Brooklyn Cares' awning got some attention as it heralded not just a new business but part of the renaissance of the area.

My former bosses had been concerned that I would take clients away from their practice but the reality is that I was much more than a few blocks away in a totally different neighborhood with an entirely different population. In fact, someone would have to pass several other veterinary clinics to get from my former clinic to my new one. However, eventually some of their clients did indeed find me. My first client was a poodle mix who needed a vaccination. I gave it for free in the hopes of establishing some good will and maybe I did, but that particular owner never came back.

Eventually the clients came rolling in and once they did I had the opportunity to adapt business practices to suit their needs. For example, despite the fact that I had designed large exam rooms designed to be welcoming, many people preferred not to wait there, so I gave them a choice by adding benches outside for their convenience and comfort so they could watch what was going on.

On the marketing side, I spent time and money on a direct marketing campaign and got only one appointment! I then switched my attention to web-based marketing and started to get a lot of great online reviews, which really helped. I also reached out into the community; I gave talks at schools and gave back to the community as you can read in the next chapter. Giving back became a big marketing strategy but also one of the prouder accomplishments of my Brooklyn Cares.

I also learned ways to address the cost issues that are common in a veterinary practice. For one thing, I didn't want to be the person talking to owners about costs. The technician would engage the owners and give them an idea of costs as well as understand what the owners what they could afford. The technicians were great at discussing estimates and trying to find ways to accommodate owners who just didn't have the money for the procedures they wanted performed. We offered Care Credit and payment plans and even bartering. And one such barter led to a unique offering.

One man had a five year-old cat that needed significant surgery and a lot of rehabilitation. He couldn't afford it but as he was in the brewing business, he offered cases of his ale in return for his cat's treatment. Cases of this ale arrived at the clinic. I gave some to my friends but I had many cases left over. So I started offering it to my clients, who appreciated the gesture. Soon we added wine to our list of giveaways!

I thought a lot about payment issues and then worked out a new type of pet insurance plan. It involved pre-certification for certain issues and if animals had a specific limiting condition, once they were treated for that problem they could be enrolled in the program. I spent a lot of time working on the details and I still have a patent on the idea. I did have twenty or so people sign up but I had to drop the idea as it was consuming too much of my time. Even great ideas can run into time traps and I tracked my time and other resources very carefully. If you are spending time and resources on projects you need to ensure that they are producing results. And that requires constant and rigorous monitoring of not just your time and activities, but that of the entire team. While this idea of treating and locally insuring patients is a great one, my time was better spent on my clinic, giving back and saving lives.

Other adaptations involved procedures for managing aggressive animals -- and aggressive owners. Some dogs, in particular, could be very aggressive and we would schedule them when no one else was in the clinic and bring them in through a special entrance so they wouldn't cause problems. For aggressive and rude owners, we would show them out of a special entrance and door, after referring them elsewhere. I won't tolerate rude and disrespectful folks and it is simply not worth having their business. They can create havoc with threats and even stupid complaints to the licensing board, which still have to be defended regardless of their merit. So I saved my staff and my sanity by not allowing them and making sure they knew that the service we provided was out of love and not to be taken lightly.

As a holistic practitioner who focused on healthy lifestyles I initially made a decision not to sell packaged dog food. This pleased my wife who was concerned about rodents, who were fairly common at that time in our area. We did sell natural herbs and I would rather educate clients about nutrition and raw foods than simply selling them packaged food. Eventually, we did start selling some packaged food to cater to popular demand, but it was still sold in the context of nutrition education and holistic alternatives. Initially, I didn't sell many other products like tick and flea medication but again, I began stocking some brands that I thought were effective and safe products. These products were sold in the context of my expert opinion and educating the clients. I was first and foremost in the veterinary business, practicing the best medicine. I was not a food or medications retailer. You always have to be mindful of the primary business you are in.

I was constantly adapting to the changing needs of the clinic and my customers. I remodeled significantly after about eighteen months because amongst other things I wanted an isolation room where I could treat infectious diseases like kennel cough. I relocated the surgical suite downstairs. In fact, this was to be the first of three remodeling projects as I adapted to the changing needs of the practice. I discovered that I could always learn more about my business and use the knowledge if it made sense.

The practice grew quickly and was soon one of the most successful clinics in Brooklyn. It had been built on a strong understanding of my clients and their needs and on the brand of excellent, holistic practice. It was built on caring about the community that we served as well as my team members who helped serve the community. It was built on making adaptations to accidental discoveries. It was built on understanding how our resources were being used and optimizing our time and our money. It was built on embracing our brand and embracing our differences. Like the aardvark, we adapted and thrived on our uniqueness.

Stories from the Wild: Speaking with Dolphins

Communication is critical in any endeavor. It is the root of teamwork and collective survival and adaptation. However, because animals communicate differently from us, in that they don't use our type of words, the assumption is that they don't communicate or if they do, only at a very simple level. But here's a delightful piece from National Geographic for Kids that suggests some animals are very effective communicators.

Dolphin Speak[1]

"Here's a conversation worth talking about: A mother dolphin chats with her baby…over the telephone! The special call was made in an aquarium in Hawaii, where the mother and her two-year-old calf swam in separate tanks connected by a special underwater audio link. The two dolphins began squawking and chirping to each other—distinctive dolphin chatter.

Cracking the Code

"It seemed clear that they knew who they were talking with," says Don White, whose Project Delphis ran the experiment. "Information was passing back and forth pretty quickly." But what were they saying? That's what scientists are trying to find out by studying wild and captive dolphins all over the world to decipher their secret language. They haven't completely cracked the code yet, but they're listening … and learning.

Chatty Mammals

In many ways, you are just like the more than 30 species of dolphins that swim in the world's oceans and rivers. Dolphins are

---

1 http://kids.nationalgeographic.com/explore/nature/secret-language-of-dolphins/#dolphin-communication.jpg

mammals, like you are, and must swim to the surface to breathe air. Just as you might, they team up in pods, or groups, to accomplish tasks. And they're smart.

They also talk to each other. Starting from birth, dolphins squawk, whistle, click, and squeak. "Sometimes one dolphin will vocalize and then another will seem to answer," says Sara Waller, who studies bottlenose dolphins off the California coast. "And sometimes members of a pod vocalize in different patterns at the same time, much like many people chattering at a party." And just as you gesture and change facial expressions as you talk, dolphins communicate nonverbally through body postures, jaw claps, bubble blowing, and fin caresses.

Thinking Dolphin

Scientists think dolphins "talk" about everything from basic facts like their age to their emotional state. "I speculate that they say things like 'there are some good fish over here,' or 'watch out for that shark because he's hunting,'" says Denise Herzing, who studies dolphins in the Bahamas.

When the going gets tough, for instance, some dolphins call for backup. After being bullied by a duo of bottlenose dolphins, one spotted dolphin returned to the scene the next day with a few pals to chase and harass one of the bully bottlenose dolphins. "It's as if the spotted dolphin communicated to his buddies that he needed their help, then led them in search of this guy," says Herzing, who watched the scuffle.

Language Lessons

Kathleen Dudzinski, director of the Dolphin Communication Project, has listened to dolphins for more than 17 years, using high-tech gear to record and analyze every nuance of their language. But she says she's far from speaking "dolphin" yet. Part of the reason is the elusiveness of the animals. Dolphins are fast swimmers who can stay underwater for up to ten minutes between breaths. "It's like studying an iceberg because they spend most of their lives underwater," Dudzinski says.

Deciphering "dolphin speak" is also tricky because their language is so dependent on what they're doing, whether they're playing, fighting, or going after tasty fish. It's no different for humans. Think about when you raise a hand to say hello. Under other circumstances, the same gesture can mean good-bye, stop, or that something costs five bucks. It's the same for dolphins. During fights, for example, dolphins clap their jaws to say "back off!" But they jaw clap while playing, too, as if to show who's king of the underwater playground.

"I have not found one particular dolphin behavior that means the same thing every time you see it," says Dudzinski. "If you like mysteries and detective work, then this is the job for you." And who knows—maybe someday you'll get a phone call from a dolphin."

This article can be found at http://kids.nationalgeographic.com/explore/nature/secret-language-of-dolphins/#dolphin-communication.jpg

Chapter Five

Rebuilding Brooklyn: How Others Found their Passions

I wasn't alone in wanting to help redevelop Fulton Street and the surrounding area. There were other entrepreneurs in different businesses who not only saw the potential but were excited about contributing to the restructuring of the neighborhood. They came from different backgrounds, with different perspectives and different ideas, but we also shared a lot in common. Here are their stories:

Sean Meenan is a guy who loves creating a great ambience for people of all walks of life to come together. A former amateur boxing champion, Sean had always worked in film and restaurants until he started opening his own cafes. In fact, he had started two under the "Habana" brand as well as co-owning a restaurant in Manhattan. When he came to Brooklyn in 2005 and saw Fulton Street he, too, saw a place where he could realize his vision. He wanted a place with open space where people from all walks of life could sit together and enjoy camaraderie and great food. Sean, however, needed imagination to see the possibilities when he saw a property for sale. The 'For sale' sign was handwritten and there was a sinkhole at the edge of the property. But Sean was able to look beyond those temporary issues and saw a venue that could house his dreams.

At first, Sean could not even get an audience with the owner who was selling the property himself. Being adaptive, Sean didn't let this deter him. He found out about the owner's habits and caught him early one morning. They started to talk and before long Sean was hanging out with the owner and his friends, several of whom were developers. Soon, there were serious discussions and one of the developers actually gave Sean the money to buy the building.

Sean has always been interested in making things better, not just for himself, but for everyone. He was fascinated by sustainability for its own sake not because he is necessarily an environmentalist. He wanted to recycle and repurpose, not just garbage, but also commodities like water. He wanted solar panels mounted not on the roof, but wanted them visible as an art form as well as an environmental statement. However, once he started he really became interested in how he could be environmentally sensitive in every aspect of his business. For example, he researched different types of cups and other utensils and generally worked hard at creating the best carbon footprint.

Sean, too, was into empathetic planning. He observed and listened to his customers' needs. His dream was an outside eaterie, which combined great food with an ambience that encouraged strangers and locals to interact and enjoy the diversity that Brooklyn had to offer.

Sean was also passionate about treating his team members well and getting them engaged with the patrons. Guys who worked in the back kitchen interacted with the customers, which generally worked very well. Within the team of employees, including management, there was also a lot of diversity. Sean's vision was of everyone working in harmony with the freedom to express themselves uniquely. In fact, freedom and creativity are the hallmarks of the Habana Outpost. It is as if people who go expect the unexpected.

The sense of harmony and diversity is created by the communal seating, which can put unlikely groups sitting together. Often these people would never sit together but in the spirit of freedom and harmony of the Outpost, these groupings create great interactions and unlikely friendships. Bikers might sit with kids, older locals with younger visitors, but the atmosphere and ethos of the place create magical moments and great connections. Sean admits that when he sees the magic working he feels that his vision is being realized. If fact, multimillion dollar companies like Etsy were created because of atmospheres like the one Sean created.

Lauren is another creative spirit and entrepreneur. She knew that she was not going to make a good employee -- she wanted freedom to experiment and be creative in whatever she was going to do. But what was she going to do? She had retired early as a ballet dancer, but loved to teach dance as well as yoga. She had also been a nanny and it was clear that her heart was in teaching, especially of younger children.  Initially, she was looking for a coop in Manhattan and her goal was to find a location that would support a business without her needing a car. She never thought she would leave the city but she started looking elsewhere.

She struck up a great relationship with a realtor in Brooklyn who soon found her a space on Columbia street with a great rent. She used her small amount of savings to lay a wood floor and started teaching dance and yoga. She actually opened her business a day after she graduated from college. She borrowed a small amount a money from her parents for initial expenses and also worked other jobs so she could realize her dream. Soon, however, she realized that she needed to expand her classes and brought in others to run different activities, Lauren was nothing if not adaptive. She eventually learned through empathetic planning that what was really needed was a pre-school. Starting small was the key to Laurens success then expanding in response to her community.

Discussing the idea with her friends around the kitchen table she really became inspired by the idea of progressive education. Now, 7 years later Lauren has two locations where she offers the latest ideas in pre-school education. Her program takes the best of established schools like Montessori and Waldorf (ideas over 100 years old) and presents learning in a new and exciting way.

Lauren, too, decided to create a sustainable, environmentally friendly atmosphere. For one thing, it was a good lesson for the students, and for another just good for the neighborhood. It was one way of giving back. Like Sean and myself, Lauren also believed strongly in treating her team with respect, trust, and opportunities. She also puts money aside for monthly team activities, such as a movie outing, a staff meal or even a wellness-related activity. Lauren is also donates her space to support community activities like a Hindu Sunday school and a place for local artists to display their work. She sees her space as a place where folks in the community can express themselves. If you ever need a space in Clinton Hill, please contact Lauren!

Tess Gill has always been into nature. Years ago she imported beautiful hand-made crafts from around the world. When she saw a space on Fulton Street she thought it would be an ideal spot to offer natural foods. She was concerned, however about the state of the neighborhood. There were homeless people and drug addicts and some stores that really were fronts for illegal activities. Tess recalls going into a candy store and not seeing too much candy around, and a couple of questionable characters in residence telling her that the store was closed.

However, she saw the possibilities and had the sense that eventually there would be a grass roots demand for natural, healthier alternatives. Working with a small budget supplemented with an SBA loan, Tess opened her grocery store, Victory Garden, with the hope that she could help make local eating habits healthier. She too, practiced empathetic engagement and before long realized there was a demand for which she was not yet fully prepared. Customers didn't want to just buy healthier foods, they wanted to eat them, right there. Tess needed to start a cafe.

Tess, too, was environmentally conscious. If you want to contribute to a neighborhood, you don't want to trash it. The environmentalism that all of us starting businesses at that time came from a desire to improve the community. And sustainability and environmentalism are eloquent messages about belonging to the community. You should see the amazing garden in front of her store.

Tess has faced numerous challenges not the least of which are other adaptive local competitor stores stocking some of her specialty items, and the challenge of running a retail and a cafe space on a limited budget. But her store has contributed to the rapid and remarkable change in the neighborhood. It has probably improved the health of her neighbors, too as several other stores started copying her local and organic vibe.

Gary was another restaurateur who saw possibilities in Fulton Street while it still housed a methadone clinic and many of its clients wandered the streets. A creative guy, Gary found a spot that would allow for his expression and desire to provide a great ambience where patrons could enjoy coffee, company and culture. He was a pioneer on Fulton Street so his cafe

Outpost is aptly named. For a while, the Outpost was literally in the middle of nowhere but it's bright exterior and landscaped interior did provide an oasis in the midst of urban decay. His high end vintage furniture and exotic plants provided a welcome counterpoint to the sometimes bleak outside.

Like all of the other entrepreneurs mentioned above, Gary built his business around the customer experience. At first he served only coffee but soon appreciated the demand for snacks and delicacies. He and his whole team made you feel so welcome, it was always a pleasure to drop in to the Outpost, where one felt safe, and transported into a different environment.

All of the above entrepreneurs recognized that their customers weren't just clients, they were neighbors, too. They recognized that they shared a responsibility for the environment and overall well-being of the neighborhood. They recognized that a business is not just there to serve the community but to also be part of the community. As a result of this acceptance of responsibility, as the businesses grew, so did the neighborhood.

Stories from the Wild:
Emperor Penguin

Acting for the good of the community is not just -- or even -- the prerogative of humans. Many species show behavior designed to collectively protect the herd. One example is the magnificent Emperor Penguin.

Collective Survival

Emperor Penguins are beautiful birds that typically are about four feet tall -- the largest of the species. They mostly live in Antartica where the temperatures can drop to -60C!!!

Another piece on the National Geographic for Kids[2] website, outlines the strategies these magnificent creatures use to adapt and survive.

"To survive in such low temperatures, these brilliant birds have special adaptations they have large stores of insulating body fat and several layers of scale-like feathers that protect them from icy winds. They also huddle close together in large groups to keep themselves, and each other, warm.

Around April every year (the start of the Antarctic winter) emperor penguins meet to breed on the thick Antarctic ice. By the time the female lays her egg (usually around June), she's worked up a big appetite! She passes the egg to the male before journeying up to 80km to the open ocean where she can feed her hungry tummy on fish, squid and krill.

During this time, the males are in charge of keeping the egg safe and warm in the breeding ground. They do this by balancing

---

2   Collectivism, Conservation; Emperor Penguins From the national geographic site for kids http://www.ngkids.co.uk/animals/emperor-penguins

the egg on their feet and covering it with feathered skin, called a 'brood pouch'. It takes about two months for the eggs to hatch.

The females return in July, bringing with them food in their bellies which they regurgitate (or throw up) for the chicks to eat. The females now take over babysitting duty, leaving the males to head to the ocean for their own fishing session."

http://www.ngkids.co.uk/animals/emperor-penguins

Chapter Six

Giving Back: Redefining Success

Throughout this book so far you have heard about my free spirit and how I valued the ability to be an independent thinker. I may have seen myself as independent in my thought but I have always appreciated how interdependent we all are on each other. From the study of eco-systems in my Hampshire environmental class, to my experiences with bigger creatures, I know that life, happiness and success is about interdependence. When you help another person you enrich two lives, theirs and yours.

It was with this spirit and ethic of interdependence that I opened my vet practice in Brooklyn and helped rebuild a neighborhood. Giving back was actually part of our mission statement. I believe that if you want to be the best you have to identify what that takes and make it a central part of your purpose that drives your actions every day.

> "Interdependence is and ought to be as much the ideal of man as self-sufficiency. We are social beings."
>
> Mahatma Ghandi

It was no co-incidence that I called my practice Brooklyn Cares. I recognized that my business was part of an environment that included people, other businesses and homes. Caring about people, animals, my whole neighborhood was very important to me and a central part of our mission. Simon Sinek talks about the "why." He argues that most businesses talk about *what* they do and *how* they do it but that misses the most important question for both the organization and its customers -- the *why*. I could tell you that we are a veterinary practice and that we take an inclusive approach to our treatment of animals. But what about the why? Because we care. It is why I called our clinic Brooklyn Cares. We did care and it manifested itself in many ways. If you don't care, or can't do it better than someone else, don't bother.

It started from the moment I designed the practice. I wanted sustainability, to create a green practice, and one way of realizing it was by using solar panels. We were the 56th building in Brooklyn to install solar panels. The panels were an obvious and visible testimony to our commitment to sustainability. We were environmentally sensitive in other ways, too. For example, we were completely paperless. We gave away tote bags rather than put things in plastic bags. We used dimmers and timers on all electrical outlets. The Green Team from New York did energy audits, which allowed us to be mindful of our consumption and to modify it where necessary.

Another way we showed we cared was by fostering animals. We would take them in and often find homes for them amongst existing clients, friends and strangers, who then became existing clients. We were part of a Rescue network that took in and then fostered out abandoned or lost animals. I loved when people offered to foster one of these animals and knew that once they fostered a rescued animal, most people would end up keeping them.

We cared about people, too. In many different ways we reached out to help and support others. For example, I wanted to give my team the best possible work experience and as much training as possible. Everyone in the clinic was trained in multiple roles. Not only did this cross-training enhance their own skillsets it made the practice more efficient. At any time, anyone could step into another role without disruption to the operation. The training became so effective both at the organizational and individual level that we extended it to kids who had dropped out of high school. In conjunction with the Cambria program, we gave kids some shape to their lives who were a bit lost and directionless.

There were a variety of teenagers who came through the program. One girl was homeless and we helped find her a place to stay. Deshawn, one of eight children, was meant to be a football hero, a star linebacker and an NFL hero. However, he badly tore his ACL in his junior year and his football dreams were over. He became depressed, his grades crashed and he dropped out. He was facing fourth and very long when he joined our clinic. He was still depressed and we had to keep on him to do his work, for example, run a lab test. We encouraged him to keep up his studies and still aim for college. He was a super kind kid with a big heart and actually very good with animals. He did eventually get a GED and we encouraged him to get his college applications together. He enjoyed working at the clinic and he decided he wanted to go to Mercy Vet Tech school in Dobbs Ferry, Westchester County in New York.

> "Giving back involves a certain amount of giving up."
> Colin Powell

Dashawn was invited for an interview and on the day in question we called him just to make sure he was ready. He sounded depressed and was making excuses as to why he couldn't go. He was going to but missed the train and there was no transportation. No one in his very large family had gone to college and he was having serious doubts. My wife and I wasted no time. We dropped what we were doing, rode over to his house and drove him an hour to his interview. We wanted to make the point that we believed in him and that there was no alternative. It was a turning point in his life.

Another of our interns was a teenager living in a foster home. She had actually got pregnant and she, too, was somewhat lost. Again, we took her under our wing and helped her a lot -- securing a nice apartment for her in downtown Brooklyn for a subsidized $300 a month. The average rent for her type of apartment in that area was six times that amount. It made a huge difference to her.

> Life doesn't make any sense without interdependence. We need each other, and the sooner we learn that, the better for us all."
> Erik Erikson

Sometimes the opportunities to help kids came in unexpected ways. On the first day of my son's second year in pre-school, I walked with him to drop him off only to find the doors were locked and there was a fairly frustrated and angry crowd of pre-schoolers and their parents outside. There was a problem with a magnetic lock and Lauren the head teacher could not get it open. Time was passing and parents needed to go off to work. I made the decision to invite all of the children back to my practice until the lock was fixed. The children seemed intrigued, the parents grateful and the teacher was relieved. Twenty kids marched with me two blocks back into the clinic and a few more joined us later. We gave them all crayons and paper and showed them the clinic. Some of them also sat in on appointments and some enjoyed switching the X-ray light box on and off! And of course, our rescue pig, Piggy Smalls, was fed about three times as much as normal. Fortunately, it wasn't a terribly busy morning and I think the kids had a blast.

I always wanted the animals and their owners to feel special and know that I cared -- which I truly did. This was shown in various ways. I often had a large accounts receivable because I would -- within reason -- give the animals what they needed regardless of whether their owners could pay. I was known for giving away vaccines because they were important to the animals. Sometimes an owner could only pay for one and then I would often give another two for free. In fact, I would often say to those clients, "you pay for the most important shot and I'll pay for the rest." I also never euthanized for economic reasons.

Now you may think that this was poor accounts management but I got back the unpaid due many times over in reputation, loyalty and referrals. Those three things are more important than any unpaid bill. In fact, one time a well-off owner baulked at paying for an expensive test, so I suggested some alternatives. She trusted me and appreciated my candor as well as my willingness to accommodate her, so in the end, she ended up spending a small fortune on alternative assessments which ended up saving her pup.

I also wanted to respect my animals and their owners' feelings when it was time for them to be euthanized. I created a Zen room, a peaceful, quiet, dimly lit place where owners could be with their animals just before and even after they had been euthanized. In the Zen room owners would hug their pets, hold them and cry with them. They would remember all the wonderful times they had spent with their animals and honor them as they passed peacefully.

Honor and respect were key components to Brooklyn Cares. I would honor the team with weekly barbecues that we would have in the back yard of our clinic. One time, we staged a Reps day where all the reps from various pharmaceutical, product and equipment companies came to join us at our backyard barbecue. It was a lot of fun, watching these competitors sitting together having a good time. It was a great opportunity for everyone to communicate and develop relationships. In fact, I was thrilled when a distinguished Vet lawyer, business consultant and mentor of mine Dr. Wilson, came all the way from Philadelphia to join us on Rep Day.

> *"Giving back is something that comes from the heart to me. It's not that I do it because it's the right thing: I do it because I want to do it."*
>
> Henry Kravis

Another simple gesture of caring came in the form of pens, beer and wine and, as I mentioned earlier, tote bags that we gave away, often in lieu of plastic bags for carrying medicines and the like. I still see those tote bags all over the place -- even in Manhattan --and I know the people carrying them aren't clinic clients.

Recognizing interdependence and the importance of the relationships with everyone -- from the animals to their owners, from my team to interns, from reps to my neighbors, was essential for the development of my business as well as my integrity. I would not have wanted it any other way. The trust and respect that we developed allowed us to be authentic and appreciated. And most of all it showed people our why.

If you want to be the best, you need to know that means not just being good at what you do and how you do it but being great at conveying why you do it, in everything you do. That's how I built the best veterinary practice in Brooklyn.

Stories from the Wild: Apes

Giving back and giving to others is empathy and emotional intelligence in action. So often people underestimate the power of animals to empathize and try to act for the good of the tribe. I love this story from Frans De Waal's delightful book *Our Inner Ape*.

Good-Natured

"The two-meter-deep moat in front of the old bonobo enclosure at the San Diego Zoo had been drained for cleaning. After having scrubbed the mat and released the apes, the keepers went to turn on the valve to refill it with water when all of a sudden the old male (bonobo), Kakowet, came to the window, screaming and frantically waving his arms so as to catch their attention. After so many years, he was familiar with the cleaning routine. As it turned out, several young bonobos had entered the dry moat and were unable to get out. The keepers provided a ladder. All bonobos got out except for the smallest one, who was pulled up by Kakowet himself.

Kakowet seemed to realize that filling the moat while the juveniles were still in it wouldn't be a good idea even though this would have obviously not affected himself."

Chapter Seven

Playing with a Ball

Vets are in the unique position of being both generalists who need to know everything about animal physiology and biology, and specialists who excel at certain aspects of veterinary medicine. Vets are also in a unique position -- they are licensed to kill.

I had my first experience with euthanasia when I was twelve years old. Rudy, my dog at the time, seemed fine one day but sick the next. He went downhill pretty rapidly. He was bleeding from his spleen, which most of the time indicates a tumor. The vet told us the prognosis was not good and it was decided to put Rudy down. Poor Rudy looked really sick and while I was, of course, sad at seeing him go, the decision and process of euthanasia seemed straightforward and clear cut. I didn't think about putting animals "to sleep" anymore -- until I got to vet school.

> *"Until one has loved an animal, a part of one's soul remains unawakened. "*
>
> Anatole France

There is very little mentioned in vet school about euthanasia, except *how* to do it. So, I really hadn't thought much about it. And then I came face to face with the issue.

In vet school I was working on the internal medicine rotation, which meant that we would see a wide variety of problems referred to the school by different vets. On this particular day, I went to meet my next client. Little did I know how important this consultation would be.

Buster was a very sweet, six-year-old, longhaired retriever with a shiny coat. He had a ball in his mouth as, tail wagging fiercely, he came up to inspect me. The problem with Buster was that his kidneys were shutting down. The owners had seen three vets in the previous four months to get an answer to the problem but the prognosis was not good. All of the vets had prescribed medications for Buster but he seemed as if he was on downward spiral. There was only way this was going to end. And the end was what Buster's owners now had in mind and wanted to discuss. They thought it was time to put Buster down and were seeking my authority and approval for the euthanasia.

I ran some tests, of course, specifically of the Blood Urea Nitrogen (BUN) that measures kidney function. The normal score was 30 but Buster's was 'at least' 400 - it could have been more but the test didn't go above 400 because at that point there was little advantage in knowing how abnormal it was. It was already deadly. I looked at Buster and had a hard time reconciling this death sentence test result with the dog that was playfully walking around with a ball in his mouth, energetically engaging me and wagging his tail.

I went to seek out my supervisor. Dr. Meryl Littman, a very thoughtful, charming, diminutive lady with a huge reputation in the veterinary world. She has done some excellent research on Lyme Disease and on various vaccines. Typically, someone in my situation would report the BUN score to the supervisor, say that the owners were looking to euthanize the dog and that would be it. It wouldn't a case of Buster, a six-year-old dog, it would be a "end stage glomernephritis" in room 4.

It wasn't that simple for me.

I explained the history of the case, but I also explained how the dog appeared to have energy and was playing with the ball. I went into some detail about how Buster had tried to befriend me. My ambivalence and confusion were clear to Dr. Littman.

"Clearly, you are having a problem with this?" she commented.

"How can you euthanize a dog that is playing with a ball?" I asked.

Dr. Littman looked at me for a second and then asked for Buster's BUN score. I told her.

She was typically thoughtful for a moment and then said, "Lots of tests show deteriorating disease. Let's ignore that for the moment. How's the dog?"

I told her again that I thought the dog, while sick, still seemed to have a lot of energy and vitality.

"If you don't want to euthanize a dog, you shouldn't. Let's go and talk to the owners," Dr.Littman said purposefully

We went into the exam room and Dr. Littman could see for herself that Buster still had some life in him. He was continuing to interact with the ball, carrying it around the room playfully. I explained to the owners that Buster's brain had adapted somewhat to his kidney condition and that his prognosis was poor but that he might still have some time.

Dr. Littman asked the owners what they were feeding Buster.

"At this stage we are feeding him anything he wants," replied the woman.

"He really loves steak," added her husband enthusiastically.

Dr. Littman pointed out that protein was the worst food to give Buster as this was contributing to the kidney disease. She recommended more carbs and some other nutritional tips.

"Should we put him down?" asked the man bluntly.

"I wouldn't euthanize a dog that was playing with a ball," Dr. Littman said, glancing in my direction.

"How will we know when it's time?" asked the man.

"All of the other vets have looked at his blood results and shaken their heads. I think they believe he should be put down," said the woman, as a hint of a tear appeared on her cheek. "When will we know?" she asked, looking directly at me.

I thought for a moment and then spoke from the heart. We hadn't been taught about this in class and the ideas just flowed naturally.

"Think of all the things that Buster loves to do. When he can't do most of them any more, it will be time."

Dr. Littman looked at me. I thought she nodded. Then she left the room.

"Thank you!" said the woman, holding back a tear.

"Yes, thank you," said the man, extending his hand in gratitude. There was a moment of connection as we exchanged glances.

"Come on, Buster!" said the woman, "Get your ball and let's go home."

It was two months later and I had left internal medicine and was now in the surgical department rotation. I had a busy day assisting in various surgeries. I was really a glorified technician in the operating room, giving the surgeon the tools he needed, cleaning up and generally just observing surgical procedure. I arrived home late, finished dinner and was getting ready for bed when I got a call from the hospital. I needed to come back to assist in some emergency surgery. Two pit bulls had gotten into a fight and they were both in bad shape. This was the first time that I had been called back late at night for emergency surgery duty.

I arrived at the hospital around midnight, barely three hours after I had left. The pit bulls had been in a vicious fight and although their injuries weren't life threatening, they both needed surgery for lacerations and other injuries that could not wait. It was going to be a long night.

The surgery went on for hours. Around four in the morning, a nurse came in to the operating area and informed me that three people had just shown up and were asking for me by name. Actually they insisted that they only see me.

The nurse could see my brow furrow in confusion.

"They have a dog called Buster with them," the nurse said looking for any sign of recognition from me.

I told the nurse I would be with them as soon as I could but it might still be an hour or two.

At around six in the morning I walked out to the waiting area. There was Buster with his owners and a twelve year old girl. They had been waiting for me for a couple of hours. Buster didn't have his ball.

We went into an exam room.

The owners hugged me and then I was introduced to their sad pre-teen, Angela.

"How has it been?" I said, knowing the answer.

"We have had the best two months with Buster!" said the woman. "We've taken him everywhere. He has had so much fun on the beach."

"I think it has been his best two months ever!" said the Angela, perking up out of her somber state.

"But now he can't do those things he used to love to do," interjected the woman. She had made a detailed list and rattled off all the things he enjoyed doing from playing with a ball, greeting Angela and eating.

Buster looked pretty sick. The energetic, lively animal I had seen just two months ago was now a distant memory.

"We know it's his time, now," said the man. "But we wanted you to be the vet who puts him down."

That was technically a problem. I wasn't yet a fully licensed vet and so I couldn't euthanize Buster. I could, however, euthanize him under supervision. I knew that a qualified vet was in the clinic and after a few more minutes left the owners and Buster briefly alone together and went to get the vet on duty so she could supervise my first euthanasia.

We all gathered in the room. The supervisor was sensitive enough to stand at the back as Buster, his family and I gathered together.

I told them that I was in no rush. "Please take all the time you need," I whispered.

One by one they hugged their beloved animal. He looked lovingly back at each of them as they cried and stroked him for the last time. They nodded their head in agreement and looked at me. It was time.

I injected Buster with a sedative then the lethal concoction. Then we stood around him, holding hands. Buster closed his eyes and slipped peacefully away as we celebrated his life.

"Thank you so much," said the woman as she gave me a hug. Angela did the same. The man shook my hand in appreciation.

Buster and his family taught me a lot about euthanasia. I never imagined that I would get so much appreciation for putting an animal down, but I realized in that instant what a critical moment it was in a pet owner's life. That difficult moment needed to be embraced and cherished.

Euthanizing animals became a passion of mine because it can be done well. In my own practice I created a separate Zen room where owners could be with their pets before and even after euthanasia to honor, respect and love their animals as they passed. And later, I more formally devised a way for owners to assess their animal's decline in the quality of life.

And I have never euthanized an animal that is still playing with a ball.

Stories from the Wild: Elephants

Grief and death are part of life and being a vet. I have always respected the process of grieving as I believe it is an essential part of being -- for both humans and animals. I love this piece by James Honeyborne that appeared in the British paper, the Daily Mail.

http://www.dailymail.co.uk/news/article-2270977/Elephants-really-grieve-like-They-shed-tears-try-bury-dead--leading-wild-life-film-maker-reveals-animals-like-us.html#ixzz3uiFDfq23

Grief in the Wild

"Perhaps the most dramatic and emotional sequence happened in our current BBC1 series, Africa, narrated by David Attenborough. We filmed an elephant mother's desperate attempts to keep her calf alive during the worst drought in 50 years in Kenya.

These animals were not dying of thirst: they were starving. Some volcanic springs were still flowing, so the animals could get water; what they couldn't get were nutrients.

By that time, the drought was well into its second year and mother and baby were trying to survive on dry twigs.

There was no hay in Kenya, there was a sense of utter helplessness, and we felt the most important thing was to document what was happening.

Cameraman Mark Deeble had been following the family for days. He saw that the mother stayed with her baby and felt she was distressed, trying to lift up the dead body and move it with her feet, before standing over the prone calf for about an hour, seeming to come to terms with the situation.

Whether you were actually there or watching events unfold on the screen, it was impossible to keep your emotions separate from what you were seeing. The mother's bereavement transmitted itself so strongly.

In a more benign environment, an elephant might mourn for longer. I have heard of animals staying beside the bodies of dead friends for three days and nights, refusing to move.

Scientists have observed extraordinary displays of emotion from elephants. When one tame animal called Abu died at a safari outfit in Botswana, his keepers brought the other elephants to say 'goodbye'. One female, Cathy, was seen crying from both eyes, tears streaming down her face.

Back in the Forties, George Adamson (the naturalist who, with his wife Joy, was the inspiration for the film Born Free) recalled how he once had to shoot a bull elephant from a herd that kept breaking into the government gardens of northern Kenya.

Adamson gave the elephant's meat to the local Turkana tribesmen and then dragged the rest of the carcass half a mile away. That night, other elephants found the body, took the shoulder blade and leg bone, and returned the bones to the exact spot where the elephant was killed.

According to Charlie Mayhew, of the Tusk Trust, elephants will 'bury' their dead, covering carcasses with branches and even taking the tusks to be placed at a different spot."

Chapter Eight:

The Incredibles

> *"Innovation distinguishes between a leader and a follower."*
> *Steve Jobs*

Before opening up my clinic, I learned that a clinic was going to be opening up before me, three blocks away. I was mortified and though about calling off the deal if I could. I called the realtor up and he said something simple but transformative. "Well I guess you just have to be better and have faith in your plan".

Success in business typically means being innovative in an established market. Establishing a totally new market is risky, and takes time. Doing what everyone else is doing in the market runs the risk of not being competitive. Being innovative and open-minded, questioning conventional wisdom and excelling at what you do is the key to success. I have already described how I and the rest of my team used these principles to set up an atypical clinic, focusing on the customer's -- both the animal's and their owner's -- experience.

It is one thing to be innovative in setting up a clinic and procedures but I also wanted to carry over creativity and out-of-the-box thinking in the treatment of my patients.

Often unconventional thinking, in retrospect, seems obvious. Hindsight makes everything obvious. For example, on the very first day we opened we got a call from some agitated animal owners. They had a problem with their python. Yep, these people actually had an eight-foot python in their home. The problem was that it had gotten out of its cage and had wrapped itself around a radiator and they couldn't figure out how to extricate it. Automatically in this situation the mind naturally goes to thinking of ways to coax, or manually disentangle, the snake from the radiator. How to do that? Then it occurred to me that the snake was attracted to the radiator by its warmth. The answer was really simple.

"Turn the radiator off," I suggested. The owners admitted that they hadn't thought of that. The python was soon back in its rightful place.

There were many times when I was asked to help with other cases where the owners were not ready to accept the advice of other vets. Often, these involved cases where other professionals had suggested it was time for beloved animals to be put down but the owners weren't ready to say goodbye and wanted another opinion.

Rosie was a German Shepherd who got into something she shouldn't: anti-freeze. She actually drank some of it and the owners rushed her to an emergency clinic. There the owners were told the grim news; her kidneys were about to fail. Treatment was a long shot and could cost as much as $20,000. This was after three hours of tests and nothing yet done.

The owners knew one of my employees and they rushed over to our clinic. The first thing I did was make poor Rosie throw up. Getting as much of the poison out of her seemed like a good idea and was the first step. We ran some tests and then I had an idea. It occurred to me that alcohol would bind to the toxic crystals and help remove them from the kidneys, mitigating their damage. I called a couple of toxicologists to run the idea by them. One of them thought it was worth a shot -- literally. One of the techs ran out to buy some vodka and as soon as she returned we set up an IV -- which we labeled 'Smirnoff.' Using hard alcohol IV is an old idea, risky but our only option to save Rosie with the resources we had. I kept checking on Rosie. Her head was tilted to one side and at first I wasn't sure whether it was a function the disease or the vodka. It turned out to be the vodka and Rosie gradually recovered and for a lot less as we didn't use top shelf vodka.

Fargo was a 17-year-old Golden Retriever who already had hip and arthritis issues. His belly was getting very distended and specialists in Florida suspected a tumor but couldn't accurately diagnose it. Several specialists there were reluctant to operate on a 17-year-old dog, especially when they were unsure of the nature of the mass. The owner was frantic for positive action and actually flew back to Brooklyn so I could help out.

I have already mentioned that, unlike many vets, I had invested in an ultra sound machine and this was one of those cases where that proved to be a very 'sound' decision. The ultra sound of Fargo's mass showed that it was unconnected to any organ. It was, in effect, a benign fatty tumor, a big lipoma the size of a grapefruit, attached only to a stalk. I aspirated the tumor and out came a lot of fat. We prepared Fargo for surgery and we removed the tumor in about two minutes. Honestly, it was one of the easiest surgeries I have ever done. Fargo lived another two years. I realize that the age of an animal will factor in a vet's decision about whether to operate and provide other treatments but that can be over-estimated and prevent the exploration and diagnosis of the underlying problem. Don't let the age of an animal blind you to the diagnosis. Old age isn't a disease.

Money is almost always an issue when an animal needs serious surgery. Bella was a lively 5 year-old Labrador and her owners weren't wealthy. They brought Bella in for an examination and it appeared that her belly was getting bigger and she was drinking and urinating very frequently. The blood work came back normal and not wanting to bear the cost of X-rays the owners were happy to take her home. My guess was that Bella had a bruise on her spleen but for now the best we could do was to keep an eye on her.

I didn't know it, but the spleen grew and before long Bella was back at the Emergency Clinic in the middle of the night. The vets there assumed it was a tumor and told the owners that surgery and the associated costs would run about $15,000, which was well beyond their means. Early the next morning the owners rushed in with Bella. I believed she needed a spleenectomy, which is big surgery usually but Bella's spleen had grown to be the size of a basketball! I made the biggest incision in my life! In fact, the spleen had pushed aside all the other organs and was dominating the abdomen. It was so large it was actually hard to remove. We had to rock Bella back and forth so we could finally remove it, but remove it we did for about a tenth of the estimated ER cost. Methodical specialist surgeons typically take much longer in surgery but sometimes the time and cost difference can be prohibitive and is not my philosophy. In surgery, knowing everything in advance can reduce surgery time while being methodical. In surgery, I limit time, trash and trauma making it as easy on the patient as possible. Bella is doing great because of it!

Fluffy was another challenging dog. He had a horrible skin rash and it was deemed that Fluffy was highly allergic. Numerous tests couldn't determine what Fluffy was allergic to, but the more important task was clearing up the terrible rash. In these situations, it's not unusual for vets to prescribe steroids, but they can have side effects. I prefer using alternative treatments, different nutrition and other natural remedies. Eventually, Fluffy's rash was brought under control but the question remained, what could he possibly be allergic to? I was curious and ran some more blood allergy tests which finally produced a positive result. Fluffy was allergic to -- rabbits. I wondered whether this was accurate and how

Fluffy could be coming into contact with rabbits. Perhaps he had been eating rabbit food? I called the owners to tell them and they burst out laughing! A short time later they e-mailed me a photo. It was a picture of Fluffy surrounded by his favorite toys -- rabbits made with real rabbit fur! It reminded me of an old veterinary truism coined by James Heriot: all animals are allergic to what they love. The owners got rid of the toys and Fluffy fully recovered.

The essence of these success stories is the ability to think outside the box (or the crate) and not just go with the obvious diagnosis and certainly to look for alternatives if the current treatment is not working. It is always important to be able to step back and view the bigger picture, something that can be problematic in all forms of medicine. With the rise of the specialists it is difficult for many vets and doctors to view a problem from outside of their particular perspective. For example, an oncologist is likely to see almost everything as a tumor. That is why the generalist is so important, they are more likely to be able to take a holistic view and that can mean the difference between life and death.

In the first year of Brooklyn Cares I ran into a particular problem, a 7-year-old cat named Patrick. His owner was a lovely elderly woman who adored her cat. But Patrick was mean and it was hard to get within a few feet of him without losing a finger. He had been diagnosed as having a urinary tract infection and had been given antibiotics. But male cats typically don't get UTIs and I was curious. I suggested that I do an ultrasound on Patrick. "Do whatever you would do for your cat," said the owner. An ultrasound might tell me whether Patrick did indeed have a UTI or was blocked in some way. We sedated Patrick which was good because the ultrasound revealed a tumor in Patrick's intestines. The tumor was a lymphoma which is normally fatal but we had caught it so early that it hadn't yet metastasized. Patrick proceeded to bite my fingers for years to come.

Olive Perez Furmuffin was a 10-year-old cat who had the classic signs of hyperthyroidism. She was throwing up and losing weight fast. Another vet had prescribed thyroid medication but after three months, Olive was not getting any better despite the fact that her thyroid levels had returned to normal. Olive revealed a truism, if something isn't working, try something else. More thyroid medicine only made Olive sicker, not fixing anything. There had to be something else going on. Eventually I found a tumor in the cat's kidney. I explained to the owner that this was a very serious problem and moreover, I had never done this type of surgery. The owner showed too much confidence in me. "Do what you can, please!" the owner said. "Please save Olive."

With my surgical assistant, Amelia, encouraging me every step of the way, and after a lot of very anxious moments, we methodically removed the tumor. The cat made a full recovery and her case is testament to the fact that you can't stop when you think you have found an easy answer if the treatment isn't working

It is humbling when owners put their animals and their trust in me. I will always do everything I can for an animal with the owner's consent and especially with their confidence in me. This was demonstrated when an artist rescued three kittens and one of them became very sick almost immediately. She brought William to me. He was just seven weeks old and probably didn't weight more than a pound. William was severely dehydrated with a bloated belly that was full of thick, yellow, sticky fluid.

The obvious diagnosis was feline infectious peritonitis, for which there is no cure. Testing would be very expensive, take days and unlikely to help. Treatments would be aggressive, expensive and would be unlikely to help for longer than a month according to most written accounts. I told the owner the sad news and even suggested euthanasia as a possibility.

"Dr. Mann, my dad is in chemo and my aunt is very sick. I believe in miracles. I need some hope. Please do whatever it takes to save William," the owner said.

Through further tests and treatment William didn't have peritonitis. He had distemper, which is rarely seen in cats. We started the cat on a regular iv antibiotic regimen. I remember checking on him every few hours, especially in the beginning when he was still in danger. He stayed with us for fifteen days and made a complete recovery. His photo is on our bulletin board Hall of Fame.

It was always amazing to watch not just animals recover but the delight, relief and joy in the owner's faces and hearts when they got their best friends back. I always would do anything I could to get make that happen.

In the next chapter, you will discover how I parted ways, somewhat expectantly, from Brooklyn Cares. Showing some differences between a small business that was run with people first verses a small business run by a bigger business far away, a dad and his young son walked in with a three pound Chihuahua puppy. The puppy had Parvo, which is normally 60% fatal. I would often give the Parvo vaccine for free because the disease is too common in Brooklyn and the vaccination is very effective. This Chihuahua needed a lot more than a vaccine. These folks didn't have the walk-in exam fee let alone the almost $2000 it was going to cost to save their beloved animal. I wasn't authorized to extend this amount of credit at this point because it wasn't my clinic but the whole clinic, including myself, was struck by how sad and helpless this puppy looked. The father and his young son looked so forlorn as they considered their options. This is hardest part of veterinary medicine. That's when I told them they could pay the fee at the rate of $10 a week until it was paid off, around 2020. Their eyes lit up and they looked so relieved and grateful. We kept the dog for three days and when he started biting us we knew he was going to be fine and ready to go home. **What we lost in revenue, we gained in love, gratitude and productivity from our clinic and worth the ire of the home office.**

I always have tried to practice a different type of medicine. I want to be thoughtful, innovative and look at the bigger picture. I want to take a holistic approach, which considers the less obvious diagnoses and treatments. I want to put the needs of my patients and their owners as my first priority. That combined with the knowledge part of aardvark method is one of the keys to business success.

I am proud of what was accomplished in a few short years. I hope you can share a similar success!

Stories from the Wild

Sometimes, as shown in this chapter, animals desperately need help from vets to heal but sometimes they heal themselves, especially in the wild. here is an excerpt from the Guardian newspaper on this subject written by Science Editor Robin McKie.

http://www.theguardian.com/uk/2003/jan/26/health.science

Animals use nature to heal themselves
"Animals wounded in the wild or stricken by disease possess a remarkable ability to treat their ailments, according to new research that has important implications for humans.

Examples of this new work include observations of capuchin monkeys that rub their fur with millipedes containing insect-killing chemicals called benzoquinones; chimpanzees who eat the pith of the plant Vernonia amygdalina to kill off intestinal worms; and domestic cats which eat houseplants or chew woolly jumpers to make themselves sick and so rid their bodies of poisons.

Even more surprisingly, scientists have found that some creatures are adept at helping people to overcome diseases. 'Dogs are particularly good at this,' said Professor Keith Kendrick, of the Babraham Institute in Cambridge. 'They have a stunning sense of smell and can detect when chemical changes occur in their owners. Dogs can tell long before the event when a person is going to have an epileptic fit. Obviously that is a talent with very important implications.'

The effectiveness of animal self-medication is also revealed in studies by William Karesh of the Wildlife Conservation Society in New York. He and his colleagues have studied a range of wild animals and found that most were in remarkably good condition.

Blood tests carried out by Karesh revealed that most of these creatures had been infected by extremely unpleasant viruses and bacteria, infections that usually kill domestic animals but which had been dealt with by their wild counterparts.

This discovery may explain why many wild animals become sick and die in captivity - because insufficient attention is paid to their living conditions.

Another example of animals' self-medicating prowess is provided by elephants which make pilgrimages to a cave complex at Mount Elgon, an extinct volcano in western Kenya. They dig out the soft rock in the cave walls, grind and then swallow it. And the reason? Sodium is a vital ingredient in stimulating bodily defenses against toxins that major herbivores will encounter in many of the plants they eat."

Chapter Nine

Business Development: Sel ing out
A Company Culture Takes over

    Every business evolves and it is ideal if you as the business owner have control over the evolution process. Part of this requires keeping track of all the important variables and being proactive in making adjustments to your practice. When I was at Hampshire College there were no tests, no grades, and very vague measures of performance. On the contrary, in my business I tracked all the important measures down to the smallest details. This was good business practice but it was also wearing. I found myself divided between being a great veterinary practitioner and being a traffic cop controlling the flow of variables that influence any business.

    Apart from formal measures there were other signs that we were a thriving, successful practice. When people stopped me on the street to thank me for the practice, when employees showed up to work every day enthusiastic and completely committed, when colleagues were complimentary, I knew that we were well-respected and successful. We had established a brand and style of practice that was appreciated, with a great reputation that stretched beyond our immediate catchment area. We were fantastic at diagnostics and holistic care. The fact that we were the number one clinic in the area for blood volume and microchips and had literally hundreds of very positive online reviews was also testimony to our reputation and excellence. When you reach that level, however, new administrative issues come up and I wan ted help.

This chapter will talk about my corporate partner and their method. I think we both agree that we used very different parameters for success and used very different methods. My method, the AARDVARK method, is outlined here and has some great aspects. Some big companies in the veterinary world use several aspects of that method. My corporate partner had several different ideas and process. While I don't agree with them, I don't ever want to be negative. They are different, they didn't work for me, but no judgement is made. Decide for yourself which methods work best for your company and let me know!

One example of a very large company that uses an empathic adaptive method to compete is VCA/Antech. Antech and Idexx are the two main companies that process blood for veterinarians. Both are great companies with wonderful labs. For awhile, they competed on price alone. I used Idexx until Antech decided to compete on something else. They came to the hospital and asked me what I wanted that they could provide. I said I wanted someone to evaluate my records and they sent a VCA founder with a ton of knowledge to talk. I said I wanted a simpler in house system and they introduced me some better machines and even arranged a lease which didn't benefit them. Through active engagement, listening to their community, this very big company earned my business.

I knew that I definitely wanted a partner that could help as we grew. But I also knew that finding a partner who was completely aligned with my practice and my values would be difficult. What was particularly difficult was finding another practitioner who was willing to admit when he or she didn't know something. In fact, I interviewed fourteen possible candidates before I found the right candidate. Dr. Stephanie Liff was a great vet who was completely on the same page as I was. We were both committed to providing great and creative medical care to our patients.

I was also interested in finding a corporate partner who could take over much of the administrative load and allow me to focus on being a vet and pursue extensions to the business. For example, I wanted a mobile website, which at the time was more complicated than it is today, as well as upgrading my existing website. I was developing a product line and different logos for various aspects of the business. Some of these creative projects couldn't really be delegated. I craved for an institutional structure that would free me from administration and business management that could easily be delegated. I started to explore various options.

The first group came and did their due diligence by doing an audit of my business. They agreed that it was very successful but were very concerned that its success was heavily dependent on my presence. They considered it a "personality" practice with too much emphasis on me which represented 'key man risk.' I understood but believe that it is critical to have that uniqueness and felt that my culture was created to be excellent, not just me. There surely is a way to marry that uniqueness with institutional structure. Another group wanted to combine practices under a new national brand. I continued my research.

I turned my attention to a smaller outfit based closer by. I drove to the company and liked what I saw. First, they manage relatively few practices but were super excited about doing a deal with me. Apparently they usually take over failing practices so I think the idea of a successful practice to partner with was new to them. The employees there looked happy, knowledgeable and engaged. They were very interested in a partnership that would allow me to draw out some equity while maintaining my role as the vet, while they took care of the administrative details.

The senior executives had put together a very well thought out plan. They nimbly and reassuringly addressed any issues that

I raised. They assured me that they would not interfere with what was working but would focus only solutions for things that could be improved. They also were going to provide profit sharing for the employees and taking care of my employees was one of my highest priorities. They extolled the virtues of a small corporation verses the bigger guys although I have since learned that size doesn't necessarily indicate great culture. In short, they did a great job of courting me. I was also encouraged that they were excited about growing the practice. They had previously taken over only practices that were struggling, which in retrospect should have been a warning sign. But my success made them even more eager to do the deal.

We talked about expanding the practice and keeping it open longer hours, from the current eight hours to twelve. I couldn't figure out how to schedule my staff so everyone was happy and they were going to make that a priority. I also had the idea of starting another practice in Manhattan, an idea that really caught my imagination and eventually consumed a lot of my time and energy. They were full of ideas and I thought I had found the ideal corporate partner.

I should have realized that we were not really a good fit on the day the deal was signed. Effectively all that happened that day was that the company came and changed out the credit card machine. It was the beginning of a change in the practice that was exactly what I feared. Corporate standardization began to replace the individual magic that all of us at the practice brought every day. Accounting concerns and practices seemed more of a priority than patient care.

Despite being seemingly enthusiastic about extending hours while we were in negotiations, the reality was that they wanted to cut employee hours, not expand them. They introduced a plan to send employees home when business was slow even though I felt that a schedule was a promise to employees. Talking of slow, simple procedures seemed to take forever, often to the detriment of the business. It was one thing for them to wait several months to provide fleece jackets for our staff, only for them to arrive with summer, but it was another to delay the payment of bills and suppliers. I simply wasn't accustomed to getting multiple disconnect notices from the utility company or to return from vacation only to find that we were out of rabies vaccination because our bill was significantly overdue. The corporation tried to explain that by not paying bills for 90 days, you had an increased opportunity to do other things with the money. Thus not paying people created more opportunity for the business. It certainly was a different approach than I was used to or believed in.

    Moreover, while I was hoping that I might get a corporate discounts on medications and supplies, we were actually now paying more for these essentials than I negotiated before going with a corporation. I think they were as much surprised as I was that they costs were in fact more before we joined them.

    As inefficiencies multiplied, morale sank. My lead receptionist was diverted to being the inventory control manager and became obsessed about counting pills, thus being lost to her main purpose. My office manager didn't like that her dream job with animals had turned into being a corporate mediator so she went back to the more corporate banking role she started with. I was shocked when I saw ten newly ordered cases of paper sitting in a closet, because we had been a paperless practice for more than three years!

    The corporate office's process was quick in wanting to fire people whom they saw as being inefficient. They would mention that their process included only keeping the best. My process didn't evaluate everyone everyday but instead took a more holistic and respectful approach. They wanted to let someone go because they didn't like how the receptionist was answering the phones. I agreed but I didn't see the need when there were other ways of handling the problem. One of my team was going through marital issues and started being late because she had to go further to get her child to day care from her mom's house than before. I wanted us to support her and encourage her in her work as I knew she was a good employee who was just going through a tough time. Corporate wanted to fire her because their process said she was no longer "one of the best". If you don't have compassion and understanding for your team members, how will you ever have it for your patients? **How will your team members support you if you don't support them?**

There was a huge disconnect between procedures and stated values, and between my values and theirs. Again, no judgements but I reached a breaking point when I was confused about interpreting a spreadsheet the corporation had sent me. When he chided me by saying "any idiot can see the tabs," I was more than annoyed. I certainly am not an idiot but I didn't see the tabs.

The tension continued to build; actually it was the only thing that was. For example, despite pre-deal enthusiasm and assurances, my mobile website was still just an idea more than a year after they had taken over. A year had passed since I had found an ideal property for a practice in Manhattan. I had worked hard to secure a 4200 square foot building on 42nd Street but the corporation now in charge of the lease took over a year to negotiate minor issues. Now, as the tension increased, the CEO assured me that while he couldn't stop me opening a practice there, he could definitely tie me up in costly legal proceedings for years. While I thought I was right and perhaps he thought he was, nobody wins when you have to fight. It was obvious that it was time to part ways.

Stories from the Wild: Flatworms in action

The conflict over control in my business and different ideas of process reminded me of flatworms. Why?

Who's in charge?
Flatworms are hermaphrodites (have both a male and female part). Who decides to get the male and female roles in mating? Sounds like some real role conflict. Who's in charge? Sounds like the perfect recipe for confusion! They actually battle it out to see who gets to be the male. The one stuck as the female gets to nurture the eggs and raise the kids while the "male flatworm" goes to the office and plays golf.

Conclusion

> *If you are going to be a garbage man, be the best garbage man you can be!*
>
> Martin Luther King, Jr.

The truth of the matter is that if you are doing what you love, you have a great chance of being successful. The secrets to the success of my veterinary practice and some of the other businesses mentioned in this book can be found in the concepts of empathetic engagement and creative adaptability. As entrepreneurs, all of us, to one degree or another, want to learn from our customers, innovate, evolve, provide excellent service, be value-driven and contribute to the community we serve. We all believe in treating our teams and customers with utmost respect. Like the aardvark, we are in a state of almost continuous evolution, which is necessary in today's rapidly transforming world. When some of these key principles got sacrificed for one reason or another, the businesses began to struggle.

My own business suffered when my corporate partner saw the practice mainly as a set of systems and standards that were driven by the bottom line. When the values changed, so did the priorities and the culture. It stopped being a center of excellence driven by passionate practitioners and a highly-engaged team that thrived on providing the best possible customer experience. There was less emphasis on activism and community participation. The relationship with my new corporate partner deteriorated to the point that it became no longer sustainable. That was when I knew it was time to leave. I wish them well and hope they have found success using their methods and processes which are so different than mine.

As I said earlier, I personally believe that the 'why' of any business is more important than the 'how.' I am all for efficiency but I don't think it can be the main reason you are in business. I was in business because I am passionate about helping owners and their animals. Of course, as well as being passionate I want to be efficient, but without the former the latter is not enough. Passion and commitment drive you to authentic relationships with customers, neighbors and team members, and that authenticity, trust and respect form the foundation on which great businesses are built.

The other businesses that opened in my neighborhood around the same time all had different types of challenges. Tessa Gill at Victory Garden faced the challenge of competition from larger supermarkets and fresh deli's in the area that started to sell similar, or in some cases the very same, holistic products. At the same time, she faced increased demand from her customers to provide prepared healthy food as well as selling like a grocery store. Her challenge was then to combine a retail store and a restaurant. She knew a lot about a grocery retail store but not too much about running a cafe. Being pulled in several directions ultimately took too much of a toll on Victory Garden. While it succeed in making a neighborhood healthier by increasing healthy options, it wasn't as profitable as hoped.

Lauren also encountered some serious challenges in running her school. Because of necessary repairs and renovations, Lauren had to close a rear door and have that back exit run through a neighboring store. In the meantime, she expanded the front entrance to include double doors, which she assumed would satisfy the regulatory need for two points of entry into the building. However, local regulators told her that because she couldn't control the back exit through the neighboring store, she didn't have the requisite number of exits. Poor Lauren. She was forced to close for three months, which was a huge financial challenge as well as a PR problem. All most people hear is that a business has been forced to close and do not make the effort to go beyond the assumptions and gossip. However, Lauren invited all the parents to see the issues, tour the spaces, and come with ideas. While some parents left because they no longer had adequate coverage, others pitched in and took kids to the playgrounds and organized groups to get through the hard times. We didn't sign up in time for Laurens children's summer camp this year. So we couldn't get in, it was oversubscribed. Lauren is opening her second location in Beacon Ny.

Sean continues to operate his outdoor Habana Outpost very successfully. However, he, too, is in transition currently falling in love and transforming New Orleans. New Orleans is lucky to have him as there is no greater creator of neighborhoods.

Our businesses collectively helped transform Brooklyn. The Clinton Hill area in particular went from a shady, marginalized neighborhood, to a sought after, fashionable place where rents can now be more expensive than Manhattan. It only takes a few people to start a movement and it's incredible what the pioneers achieved in turning the Brooklyn brand around. One person alone can't do it, but a group of entrepreneurs who are prepared to put their time, energy, money, creativity and passion into it, can create remarkable change. In the end it wasn't just our businesses that evolved it was the entire community.

In deference to the admirable aardvark, I have formulated a business model based on the experiences described in this book and, as mentioned earlier my eight point plan creates the acronym AARDVARK! The eight strategic points are **A**daptation, **A**ctivism, **R**espect, **D**rive, **V**alues, **A**nalysis, **R**eview and **K**nowledge.

In the next section of this book, there is a short workbook that will identify these key areas, ask you very specific questions about how you do or do not currently implement these strategies, and provide some action steps to get you moving in the right direction.

As you have read, my own experience in finding suitable professional, individual partners as well as corporate ones, is testimony to how critical it is that partners are fully aligned on the crucial aspects of the business as defined by the AARDVARK model. If you and a potential partner are not completely aligned on both the importance of these variables and how to implement them, you almost certainly shouldn't be working together.

I believe that the AARDVARK model addresses the core issues of a successful business and what leaders and entrepreneurs need to aspire to.

The Entrepreneurial Aardvark
8 ways to build a successful business

*Don't be an ass, ostrich, leech, snake, shark,
Do be a lion, elephant, dolphin,*

ADAPTATION:

Survival is about adaptation and so is business. In my own example, you have read that I physically renovated my practice three times in a fairly short period to make the space more efficient, allowing me to provide the best possible customer experience. I have also provided several examples when I would not accept the standard diagnosis or even the opinions of other professionals and by thinking outside the box came up with different, sometimes life-saving, solutions.

To be a successful business you need to constantly evolve and adapt to the macro and micro environment. This translates into the need to be innovative and not practice the status quo in everything you do. It means questioning everything.

Stanford psychologist Carol Dwerk writes about the difference between a growth mindset and a fixed mindset. You need a growth mindset. It allows you to question assumptions, recognize oversimplified thinking and be more efficient in order to develop a competitive edge.

It also means that you don't assume you know what your customers want, you find out what they want and how you are perceived.

Questions:

Can you anticipate local and national trends that would affect your business? Identify them. What can you do about them?

_____

_____

What sources are there for you to get customer feedback about our business? Do you use them all? What do you do with the information?

_____
_____

How does a complaining customer inform your business and what can you do about it?

_____
_____

If someone were to immediately come in and make your business better, what would they do?

_____
_____

Why do people go to your competition?

_____
_____

How often do you review systems, procedures and standards? Who does that and what action follows?

_____
_____

What would put you out of business?

_____
_____

Actions:

ACTIVISM:

As you have read, I was heavily committed to supporting and improving my community in various ways. I invested in environmentally sensitive practices - you might recall we were the 52nd property in Brooklyn to install solar panels. As well as being environmentally aware, I also provided internships, some free services, seminars, generous payment plans, as well as allowing some community organizations to use my space. I lived over my practice and so was very immersed in the neighborhood, which was very important. In fact, if you have a local service business like my veterinary practice, you would be well served by living in the neighborhood.

Whether you live there or not, you are part of your community and it will respond to you if you are engaged with them. Just providing the neighborhood with another service or place to purchase products is not a competitive advantage because anyone can, and will, do that. The business that builds trust and relationships with the community by serving it will also benefit from reciprocal appreciation.

Activism is more than just advertising; in fact it really isn't even advertising. It shows your purpose is not just making money off the people in your neighborhood, it is also about giving to the neighborhood.

Questions:

What ways is your business involved in activist activities?

_____

_____

What ways could your business be involved in your community?
_____
_____

In what ways are your competitors involved in activist activities?
_____
_____

What causes are you passionate about?
_____
_____

What causes are related to your business?
_____
_____

There are various ways in which you can actively engage in your community.

List of possibilities:

- Environmental: recycling, energy conservation
- Community: interns, free services for some, serving on community boards,
- Information: talks, seminars, pamphlets
- Facility: giving other community groups use of your facilities,
- Money: sponsorship, charity, generous payment plans and fee-reductions for those who can't afford to pay immediately, or at all.

Action:

Ensure that you do at least one action from each category in the above list of possibilities. To help you, write down what you already do, or will do, in each of the categories:

_____
_____
_____
_____
_____
_____
_____
_____
_____
_____
_____
_____

Environmental:

Community:
_____
_____

Information:
_____
_____

Facility:
_____
_____

Money:
_____
_____

RESPECT:

The story of my first experience with euthanasia described in chapter 7, is a good example of a respectful interaction based on emotional intelligence, empathy and authenticity -- the key ingredients to developing respectful relationships. In that circumstance you may recall that, despite my inexperience, I was not only empathic with the owners but authentic in my views, which allowed us to reach a mutually acceptable and satisfying solution. The authentic relationship was so respectful that when it was time to put Buster down the whole family came to seek me out personally and wait for me so I could be the one to finally euthanize their dog.

Respect is one of the fundamental requirements of any successful relationship. With respect comes trust and greater chances of the emotional connection that is so critical for a successful business. The respect has to run throughout the organization, both between team members and between the team and the outside world. Respect is a critical part of team member engagement without which you cannot excel.

Respect involves having a caring attitude about another's wellbeing, providing support and being open to their opinions and feelings. Respect also means showing you care about your team members by such things as; providing them the resources and support they need to fulfill their roles, giving them opportunities for professional development, acknowledging their contributions, making them feel engaged in the work process, etc., etc.

At the heart of respect is emotional intelligence and the ability to be empathic. You need to be able to identify what others are feeling and respect them rather than judge them. Understanding another person is not the same as agreeing with them or even tolerating his or her behavior. It is the ability to understand what you and others are feeling and manage those feelings appropriately by not letting them get in the way of rational decision-making. For example, euthanasia is a very important part of my business and I am always sensitive to the needs of the animals and owners alike.

The other central aspect of respect is authenticity. You won't gain respect if people don't believe you and see you as insincere. Sometimes, in these days of political and professional correctness, it can be difficult to be authentic but it is crucial if you want to be respected and taken seriously. Authenticity won't be achieved in an organization that doesn't reinforce it and, on the contrary, punishes people for speaking openly. If you don't have authenticity there will be no respect or trust and you will have a culture of whispers and silence, which will be incredibly destructive to your business.

Respect involves listening with the intent to understand. When you respect your customers they will respect you. Reciprocal respect = reputation.

Questions:
Are all your team members respectful of each other?
_____
_____

Have you created a culture of respect? If not, how are you going to do that?
_____
_____

How do you deal with customer complaints?
_____
_____

How do you show respect to your team members?
_____
_____

How good a listener are you? How good at listening are you various team members?
_____
_____

Are you team members emotionally intelligent?
_____
_____

Are you authentic?
_____
_____

Do you have authentic meetings were team members can feel free to air their views honestly without fear of retribution?
_____
_____

Action:

DRIVE:

As a leader you have to drive your business. The energy, passion, drive, come from you. You can't delegate those critical things. You don't have to be the smartest person in your business, and there may be others who know how to do some things better than you, but you are the driving force.

To effectively use drive, you have to know exactly what your business goals and plans are. You can be the busiest person in the world and achieve nothing. You've heard of the difference between working smarter and working harder -- ideally you do both.

Questions:

What does drive mean for you?
_____
_____

How do you manifest drive?
_____
_____

Do others in your organization see you as a driving force?
_____
_____

If you weren't driving your business forward, who would be?
_____
_____

How do you sustain drive when you're not there?
_____
_____

Action:

VALUES:

I hope that my values have become clear as you have read my story. My values are about providing the best possible care for my owners and their pets as well as being actively involved in supporting my community. My values are based on respect and compassion for my clients and my neighbors and to develop a center of excellence that serves them well. I have worked hard to ensure those are indeed the values that we practice not just talk about.

The fact is that the values of your business aren't what you say they are, they are what you actually do. The Values are critical as a driving force behind your organization, around which systems, standards and procedures are developed and implemented.

Your values also reflect your why -- the main purpose of your business that is beyond making money (if you don't have a purpose beyond making money, reconsider your business model).

For example, is your organization a meritocracy or riddled with favoritism? One measure of an organization that actually practices good values is employee turnover. Typically, employees flee an unfair and biased culture, while they stay loyal and engaged in a fair and respectful one.

As outlined above, activism should be an important part of your values, and your commitment should be obvious by the actions you take.

Questions:

What is your mission statement?
_____
_____

Does your mission statement reflect what actually happens in your business?
_____
_____

How would your clients describe your values?
_____
_____

Is your organization a meritocracy?
_____
_____

Action:

ANALYSIS:

In my business I was constantly looking at different metrics of systems and performance, gained from various perspectives, from gratuitous comments to formal evaluations.

In order to adapt and innovate as well as implement many of the aspects of AARDVARK you have to know what is going on; going on in your organization, going on in the minds of your customers, going on in your competitors' businesses. In order to find out this information you need to be set up to collect and analyze the relevant data on a consistent basis.

Here you have to know something about logic, statistics and data, specifically sample size. One negative client is not a data set -- but neither is one positive client. It is very easy to take a positive comment as a sign that your business has a great reputation and maybe it has, but you need to hear it from more than one person.

There are various ways of collecting data:

- ensuring your team is asking your client's questions about their needs, wants and how well they are being serviced by you

- formal surveys that enquire about the customer experience

- performance data in terms of variables like sales, efficiency, etc.

Constant analysis is not just or even a financial exercise, its a performance exercise. Your team are arguably your biggest asset; how of ten do you review and analyze the team process and performance?

Questions:

What aspects of your business, apart from financial numbers, do you review on a regular basis?

_____

_____

Do the data you gather inform change?

_____

_____

How could you improve your systems and procedures analysis?

_____

_____

Who in your organization is responsible for data collection on systems and standards? Customer service?

_____

_____

Do you work on the team as well as on your other assets, like equipment?

_____

_____

Actions:

RESOURCES:

A successful organization makes maximal use of all of its resources. The main resources are: time, energy, focus, money, people, physical equipment, and information. The effective allocation of resources at both a personal and organizational level is a key to success.

One of the reasons I sought out a corporate partner was that I wanted to devote my time and energy into the development of the business and delivering exceptional care rather than running administrative operations. Running standard operations was not an effective use of my resources. As it turned out, I saw my corporate partner's resource allocation as inefficient, for example, the use of a receptionist to manage inventory.

Resources also apply to your clients. There are ways that you can empower your clients so that they have the resources they need. For example, as a vet, I was always providing clients with information they needed to make the best decisions for their pets.

Questions:

How well do you do personally in managing the following resources?
- money
- time
- energy

_____

_____

How well do each member of your organization do in managing their resources?

_____

_____

How do you track and analyze employees use of his or her resources?

_____

_____

How could you improve the optimization of your resources of time, money and energy?

_____

_____

What resources do you give, or make available, to your customers?

_____

_____

Action:
Make a list of your resources. How can they be optimized?

KNOWLEDGE

If you want to have a center of excellence, you must have state-of-the-art knowledge. It might not always be possible to have state-of-the-art technology but there's no reason why you and your team should lack for the best and latest information in your field. With so much online information, including courses, it is relatively easy and inexpensive to keep up with the newest developments in your field, and all of those areas relevant to your organization, like marketing, social media, and customer service.

The provision of knowledge extends beyond just your team but also to your clients as well. Whatever field you are in, there is a wealth of information that can help your clients and potential customers make better decisions and understand relevant key processes and behaviors. In my business, that meant providing information about many aspects of pet health, like nutrition, in different formats; brochures, talks, website information and so on.

The provision of information and enhanced training of your team will increase their engagement because you are giving them opportunities for personal and career development. The provision of knowledge to your potential customer is developing a relationship with them, on which loyalty is built.

Questions:

Do you provide knowledge, or opportunities to acquire it, to your team members?

_____

_____

How much time do you set aside for your own knowledge acquisition?

_____

_____

How do you ensure that new knowledge influences business practices?

_____

_____

Do you provide knowledge for the general public? If so, what form does it take?

_____

_____

How could you improve your knowledge acquisition and provision?

_____

_____

Action:

_____
_____
_____
_____
_____
_____
_____
_____

About the Author

Dr. Mann is a native New Yorker who's lived all over the globe exploring his passions. He has worked on a large number of animals -- big and small. These escapades include birthing 100 sheep a day in the ranges of Idaho, doing lameness exams on horses in Ireland, spaying and neutering dogs on native American reservations in Utah, examining cows in Cuba, cleaning out ear mites in Honduras, providing environmental enrichment to sloths at the zoo and keeping your best friends healthy in New York City.

Dr. Mann's wide range of activities and commonalities in medicine sparked an interest in holistic treatments. This spark continued with the certification in veterinary acupuncture awarded by the Chi Institute as well as an understanding of various herbal and glandular therapies which can be used in addition to conventional western medicine to make sure you and your best friend will be happy and healthy for a long time.

Dr Mann is available for speaking engagements about a wide range of topics and can be reached at drmann@gramercyvet.com or by calling his new clinic, Whole Health Veterinary Hospital located at 335 First Ave, NYC NY 10003 phone number 212 674 0111.

www.ingramcontent.com/pod-product-compliance
Lightning Source LLC
Chambersburg PA
CBHW030811180526
45163CB00003B/1232